THE
SPIRIT
AND
THE
CONGREGATION

Studies in 1 Corinthians 12 – 15

RALPH P. MARTIN

GRAND RAPIDS, MICHIGAN
WILLIAM B. EERDMANS PUBLISHING COMPANY

IN MEMORY
OF
A DEAR CHILD

MEGAN MARIE
(August 20, 1982–July 30, 1983)
Who spoke only as an infant,
but who one day
will be raised immortal

(1 Corinthians 13:11; 15:52)

Copyright © 1984 by Wm. B. Eerdmans Publishing Company
255 Jefferson Ave. S.E., Grand Rapids, MI 49503

Library of Congress Cataloging in Publication Data

Martin, Ralph P.
The spirit and the congregation.

Bibliography: p. 155
1. Public worship — Biblical teaching.
2. Bible. N.T. Corinthians, 1st,
XII-XV — Criticism, interpretation, etc.
I. Title.
BS2655.P89M37   1984   264   84-10213

ISBN 0-8028-3608-9

CONTENTS

ABBREVIATIONS

ET   English Translation
NIV   New International Version (1973, revised 1978)
RSV   Revised Standard Version (1961 ed.)
ad loc.   at the place of the text
op. cit. in the book quoted
KJV   King James (Authorized) Version
LXX   The Old Testament in Greek, known as the Septuagint
Moffatt   *A New Translation of the Bible* by James Moffatt (revised ed.
          New York: Harper & Brothers, 1935)
NEB   New English Bible (1970)

The biblical citations are normally taken from the NIV (*New International Version*), but occasionally the author has made his own rendering, especially in the translations that precede each chapter's exegesis. The Greek text followed is that of Nestle-Aland[26] with an eye kept on the United Bible Societies' text[3] and *A Greek-English Diglot for the Use of Translators,* 1964.

FOREWORD

A book like this deserves a word of explanation to justify its existence and its claim upon a prospective reader's attention. At first glance it looks to be a series of expository Bible studies on one of Paul's letters, and it draws gratefully on the standard and current commentaries. It is also born out of several convictions. Of the many pressing issues that clamor for notice in church meetings and study groups today, one item at least stands near the top. That is, whatever we as church-folk can do to improve the quality of our public worship and give its practice a clear rationale is bound to lead to a renewal of the people of God in our time. Ministers and church leaders will therefore be alert to a passage such as 1 Corinthians 12–15 where Paul's treatment of divine worship is detailed and informative.

Even if we wanted to ignore the force of these chapters, the present-day charismatic movement will not permit that neglect. Those in mainline churches keep being nagged by neo-Pentecostals to take a fresh look at "Paul's writing to a charismatic community," with the implication intended that we should then borrow a leaf out of their book and all become "charismatics."

But all was not well at Corinth; hence Paul's serious and searching critique of what passed for Christian worship in that church. Can we identify more closely what it was that lay at the root of the trouble at Corinth? Was it just an outbreak of general disorder? Or a social stratification that alienated the poor in the congregation from the rich members? Or a failure to grasp the simple courtesies of good manners and decorum, as when (it is sometimes said) "tongues" had got out of hand, or women would interrupt the services with their chatter and were bidden to silence?

I do not think these answers go deep enough. At the heart of the Corinthian problems was an *underlying theological error* that may be stated like this: an influential group in this hellenistic church had taken hold of the notion that their baptism was their resurrection to new life; that this experience gave them entrée to an exalted life here and now; that the genius of the Christian life was for them a sensible experience of "spirit," of which "speaking in (heavenly) tongues" was the sign and proof; that this glow of spiritual energy was essentially private and personal; and that the future hope of resurrection in a new bodily existence was—for them—collapsed into a spiritual ecstasy to be enjoyed in the present.

The pages that follow will try to set this account of the Corinthian malaise on a firm basis in exegesis. But more is at stake, if the case is made out.

If Paul's analysis of the scene at Corinth and his attitude toward it has been adequately pinpointed, the lessons for us today are far-reaching. We can now understand how glossolalia was a Corinthian phenomenon, with which Paul identified himself only with extreme caution and circumspection. We can appreciate how his much-disputed teaching on "women keeping silent" in church related specifically to a local situation. We can relate his insistence on "the resurrection *of the body*" to a pastoral and pressing need to distinguish between our present bodily existence doomed to run its course into dissolution and disappearance and the Christian's hope of a new existence in a life beyond death.

The following questions vex alert pastors and Bible students today: What should we make of the modern Pentecostal/charismatic claim to "speaking in tongues," namely, that such a "sign" is a hallmark of authentic Christianity, when it appears that glossolalia at Corinth arose as an eccentricity open to serious abuse and stemming from a "realized eschatology"? What should we do with Paul's apparently severe words to women who would engage in a ministry of public speaking in a service of worship? Are these gifted women to be debarred as women (a viewpoint Paul did not otherwise share) or more likely as Gnostic teachers? What should we hold out as a Christian hope for life after death? Why is there innate resistance to (say) cremation if Christians are to believe that this "body" goes to dust following death? If so, what is the phrase, "I believe . . . in the resurrection *of the body*" doing in the creed?

Finally, I return to the question that has haunted me in preparing these studies. If one verse (1 Cor. 14:26) enshrines an apostolic dictum—that all church members have, with their individual contributions, a part to play in worship—why is public worship in the mainstream denominations so obviously at odds with the Pauline rubric? Do we need to understand Paul's writing in another way?

This book began as talks given to several church groups, and I am grateful for the stimulus and encouragement of these various contexts. The invitation to give the Derward W. Deere Lectures at the Golden Gate Baptist Theological Seminary, California, in October 1982 enabled me to put the thoughts into written form, and I pay tribute to the warm hospitality of the Dean, the faculty, and the students of that institution during a memorable week. One lecture (on 1 Cor. 14) was delivered at the annual meetings of the Society of Pentecostal Studies in November 1982, and while I have not the temerity to believe that many or any in the audience were persuaded, I can acknowledge the charity expressed in the questions raised. And, finally, preparing these studies for a course of lectures and discussions on "Exegetical Method and Practice" at Fuller Theological Seminary has sharpened my thinking and prompted further reflection.* The book as it is sent out to a wider public desires only to promote reconsideration of some live concerns not only in exegesis but in church polity and practice that we sometimes shy away from out of a timid reluctance to engage in controversial dialogue with those from whom we differ.

I am happy to acknowledge the assistance of Erwin Penner who, in the final days of his doctoral studies as my *promovendus,* cast a critical eye over the typescript, and Evelyn F. Dugan who gave me unstinting secretarial help.

Fuller Theological Seminary   RALPH P. MARTIN
June 1983

---

*This fact explains the measure of pedagogical repetition the author has allowed himself in stating Paul's argument as well as the presence of the sections headed "Points to Ponder."

INTRODUCTION

There are several reasons why 1 Corinthians 12–15 claims our attention and invites our interest. First, in these chapters *Paul's teaching on the church* is set in a context of realistic situations involving the men and women of Corinth. Often we view Paul's churchly teaching as just that, namely, part of his ecclesiology. When this happens, we tend to remove the picture of the church from concrete situations dealing with real people and etherealize it as abstract "doctrine" unrelated to the specific pastoral problems confronting the Corinthian church. As an antidote to this abstraction called "the church," Paul's discussion in these chapters will recall us to the throbbing, pulsating, often erratic life of that mix of humanity that made up "the church of God that is in Corinth." [1]

What it means to be the "church of God" in our day is one of the foremost items on the theological agenda. For a lot of Christian people the very idea of the church raises problems of identity and definition. Obviously Paul's treatment of this theme has nothing to do with our denominational divisions and groupings, though we know that the house churches at Corinth were plagued by unholy rivalry and deep social stratification. [2] Cries of party allegiance based on adherence to the leading apostolic figures were common: "One of you says, 'I follow Paul'; another, 'I follow Apollos'; another, 'I follow Cephas'; still another, 'I follow Christ'" (1 Cor. 1:12; cf. 3:22; 1 Clem. 47:3). [3] Distinctions based on social snobbery were most painfully seen at the Lord's table where the rich and the poor found themselves separated and mutually hostile (1 Cor. 11:18–22). Within this community, ethical issues led to dissension and both letters to and visits by Paul told of those matters of moral concern that had rent the Corinthian assembly.

But the issue of the church that makes it a problematic one today is the suspicion in some people's minds that the church has betrayed both its Lord and his message across the centuries. The movement that bids us to get "back to Jesus" contains the implicit accusation that the contemporary church stands in the way and threatens to act as a roadblock on that journey. According to one assessment,

> Nothing in the contemporary scene is more striking than the general regard which is felt for Jesus Christ, and the general dislike of the organized church which bears His name.[4]

That "dislike"—as Stephen Neill calls it—is thought to be explained by all that "the church" has or has not done to portray the authentic spirit of Christ throughout two thousand years. Critics of the institutional church are not slow in exposing the hollowness, hypocrisy, and lethargy of what passes for Christ's representative on earth; and no one has done so more bitingly than Søren Kierkegaard:

> Whereas Christ turned water into wine, the church has succeeded in doing something more difficult; it has turned wine into water.[5]

The "sickness" of modern Christendom poses our problem. We need to make some searching self-diagnosis, to examine our condition. The church at Corinth had *its* symptoms of malaise, which were perhaps more its exuberance and enthusiasm (see 1 Cor. 1:7; 14:12) than its lethargy and deadness; but Paul's admonition to them is just as appropriate when addressed to us as we wrestle with our identity problems in the modern world: "Examine yourselves to see whether you are in the faith; test yourselves" (2 Cor. 13:5).

Paul's readers and addressees were not, however, confronted with a challenge and left to their own resources as they tried to meet it. The second reason why these four chapters of First Corinthians have special interest is the insight they offer into *the role of the Holy Spirit in the church, and in particular his office as leader in public worship.* Both the work of the Spirit and the theology of Christian worship are matters high on the theological agenda in our time. There is no doubt that both themes are intimately related, and Paul can bring both together in one limpid statement: "we worship by the Spirit of God" (Phil. 3:3). What is not always clearly seen is that the Spirit and worship are related as problem and solution—but in reverse order. The problem posed is not so much what is to be included in any full-orbed pattern of the corporate worship as the way in which modern Christians understand and practice the leadership of the Spirit in their united worship. At Corinth the difficulty lay in giving to "spirit" too prominent a role; therefore Paul has to offer certain controls by which this overzealous abandon to "spirit" was to be regulated and channeled into more profitable ways. As we shall see, Paul's directions are governed by one ruling axiom: let all exercises of worship in the public assembly serve to promote the upbuilding of the entire congregation. His attitude toward Corinthian problems is somewhat ambivalent. While granting and applauding the rich and variegated spiritual life of the Corinthian community as they met together, he points out danger-spots when (*i*) private religious experience is made the objective of worship, and (*ii*) there is no attempt made to conserve the *koinōnia,* fellowship, uniting the different church members who are otherwise split off into many groups. The action of the Holy Spirit who is above all the spirit of unity (1 Cor. 12:12, 13) as well as the driving force in making Christian praise and prayer real and authentic is a necessary factor if Christian worship is to be all that it can and should be: "the most momentous, the most urgent, the most glorious action that can take place in human life," according to Karl Barth.[6]

A third reason for our giving heed to 1 Corinthians 12–15 lies in *the picture the passage gives of Paul the pastor.* Writing with an eye on his work as church-planter and apostle at Corinth, Paul spoke of the "daily . . . pressure of my concern for all the churches" (2 Cor. 11:28). No church gave Paul more concern than this tempestuous and motley company of the Lord's people at Corinth. He viewed them in a double light. On the one hand, like a solicitous parent he expresses great affection for his "children" (1 Cor. 4:14, 15). He calls them "my dear children," and later writes endearingly of the way his affections are moved as he seeks to remove their antagonism toward him (2 Cor. 6:11–13; 7:2). Yet, on the other hand, he expresses a deep anxiety over their state, and calls for an obedience to his apostolic counsel (1 Cor. 4:21). The term translated "concern" (NIV, 2 Cor. 11:28) is perhaps a key to Paul's ambivalence. Of his love for this congregation there is no doubt; nor is it disputed that he lavished time and energy on this pastoral assignment when lesser persons might have abandoned the case as a "loss" (see 2 Cor. 7:9, which implies that if Paul had not returned to Corinth at the height of the disaffection, the result would have been a loss [*zēmia*] to the church there). Paul's relations with this often disappointing and recalcitrant community were marked by an amazing tenacity and persistence. The tribute he pays by his citation of the "Hymn to love" ("Love is patient . . . always hopes, always perseveres"; 13:4, 7) was confirmed and illustrated by his own pastoral dealings with the very people who would read these stately words.

The obverse side of the coin is that as Paul opened his heart to reveal a deep-seated "anxiety" (*merimna*), so in 1 Corinthians 12:25 he requires that in the body of Christ where all members find a place, each part should have "equal concern"—the verb is *merimnan*—"for each other." Paul can certainly call on his apostolic "authority" since he has all the marks that accredit him (2 Cor. 12:12); but it is an authority given him to build up the congregation, not tear it down (2 Cor. 13:10), and that implies an authority to be exercised in love that "appeals" (2 Cor. 13:11) and seeks to enlist the active cooperation and goodwill of its hearers.

The same note of pastoral solicitude, then, may be expected to run through these chapters, and if it does, the model of Paul as a "minister of Jesus Christ" will become clear. And that would be an additional justification for studying these verses, since the nature of apostolic authority and the role and function of the minister/clergy in the church are two matters of great importance and continuing debate today.

1 CORINTHIANS 12:1–11

Translation

1–3 Concerning *spiritual gifts,*[a] brothers, I *do not want you to be uninformed.*[b] You know that, when you were pagans, you were led away to dumb idols, as you were *continually led.*[c] Therefore I make known to you that no one speaking by the Spirit of God says "Jesus *be* damned!" and no one can say "Jesus *is* Lord!"[d] except by the Holy Spirit.

4–7 There are varieties of spiritual gifts, but the same Spirit. There are varieties of kinds of service, and the same Lord. There are varieties of divine power at work, and the same God who is at work *in every way*[e] in all persons. To each person *is given*[f] the revelation of the Spirit for the good of everyone.

8–11 To one the speaking of wisdom *is given* through the Spirit, to another the speaking of knowledge, in accord with the same Spirit, to another *faith,*[g] by the same Spirit, to another spiritual gifts of healing by the same Spirit, to another working of miracles, to another prophecy, to another ability to distinguish between spirits, to another *different* kinds[h] of tongues, to another interpretation of tongues. All these are the work of the one and the same Spirit, who distributes them *variously and individually*[i] to each person as *he*[j] chooses.

Points to Ponder

a. τῶν πνευματικῶν: Is it better to take this as personal ("spiritual people," as in 14:37) or neuter ("spiritual gifts" [δόματα], "gifts" to be understood)?

b. A technical phrase for "reminder" (cf. Rom. 6:3).

c. ἄν here is iterative (Moulton, *Grammar,* i, p. 167) or else ὡσάν is one word "as it were."

d. No verb in these exclamations, so it must be decided whether they are statements or wishes.

e. τὰ πάντα can be adverbial (as in 13:7; 15:28; "in all ways") or substantive ("all these effects").

f. δίδοται "is given" by God. This is the use of the divine passive.

g. πίστις, "faith," can also mean "faithfulness" as a virtue (Gal. 5:22) or "wonder-working power" (Mark 11:22).

h. ἕτερος is often contrasted with ἄλλος (as in Gal. 1:6), but not in every instance.

i. An attempt to put into good English Paul's cryptic ἰδίᾳ ἑκάστῳ.

j. A key question: Who is the subject of βούλεται?

CHAPTER ONE

THE CHRISTIAN'S LORD AND SERVICE

INTRODUCTION

As we have noticed, the really important question regarding the church has to do with definition. First Corinthians 12:1–11 highlights three issues to help us understand how to recognize the *gestalt* of the church in a way that transcends culture and local convention. What are the "marks" of the church that are observable in the truly ecumenical sense? That is, granted the "church"—by derivation of the term—relates to living persons (not buildings, institutions, forms, hierarchies—all needful expressions for the church's existence and continuance in the world as a social force, however), how may an observer recognize who these people are? And what would they be doing at that point of recognition? Paul provides us with three clear parts to the configuration of the "church" when the term comes down to reality and expresses itself in human society and as a divine-human activity.

THE CHURCH LIVES BY CONFESSING CHRIST

The opening paragraph (12:1–3) sets the scene in regard to both its audience and its ambience. "I do not want you to be ignorant" is Paul's idiomatic expression by which he reassures his readers about a teaching that is part of the Christian tradition (1 Cor. 10:1; Rom. 6:3, 16). But also it is Paul's partial reply to an implied question in the letter they had sent to him. The introductory "concerning" (*peri*) continues the series of Pauline answers to a set of issues raised by the Corinthians themselves (see 7:1; 8:1). Exactly what was the subject of the inquiry to which Paul is responding is determined by how we construe the term (*peri*) *pneumatikōn*, literally "spiritual." It may be equally masculine or feminine ("concerning persons endowed with spiritual gifts," as in 2:15; 3:1; 14:37) or neuter ("concerning spiritual gifts," as in 9:11; 14:1). There are several factors that tip the scales on the side of taking the reference to be to "spiritual gifts." One is the fuller treatment given in 14:1 ("eagerly desire *pneumatika*"), which can only relate to gifts, not persons; then *pneumatika* and *charismata* (in 12:4) seem to cover the same ground but with some differentiation possible, although both refer to "qualities" or "ministries," not people. Finally, Paul's context decides the issue in that he is not talking about types of persons but is answering the question concerning the ordering of public worship at Corinth. The burning issue there was what parts of corporate worship ought to be given priority. The Corinthians evidently favored the claims of the glossolalic gifts ("tongues" and their "interpretations"). Paul is being asked to endorse this preference.

So Paul takes up the matter of "gifts of the Spirit" (*pneumatika*), which he then proceeds to set within a larger framework of God's gifts-in-grace (*charismata*; v. 4). The distinction seems clear that while the latter term is broader, referring to all manifestations of "God's grace finding particular and concrete actualization," as John Goldingay (following E. Käsemann) describes *charismata* (used sixteen times by Paul),[1] the term *pneumatika* more narrowly delimits the scope of God's gift to the exercise of that gift in public worship. As John Koenig writes, "*Pneumatika*, then, are charismata meant to be practiced within the context of congregational worship."[2] Both terms are personal and intended for congregational growth. But while *charismata* (in Rom. 12:6-8; 1 Pet. 4:10, 11, as well as 1 Cor. 12:4-11) relate to the service of the church and are linked with persons who are thus endowed, the more narrowly focused *pneumatika* describe the ingredients of a liturgical service. Thus the question raised in 1 Corinthians 14:26 is precisely the one to which Paul addresses the section of his letter from 12:1 to 14:40. The *pneumatikos* of 14:37 is one of those called to exercise gifts of the Spirit in the conduct of divine worship and to promote the ordering of that worship to ensure growth and harmony (14:26, 40).

The ambience of the passage, then, is one vital key to its meaning. Obviously all was not well within the Corinthian assembly when it "came together" (the thought recently introduced by Paul at 11:17, 18, 20, 34 with the verb *synerchesthai*, "to assemble"; it links with the phrase in ch. 14, *en ekklēsia,* "in the assembly"). The behavior at the Lord's table was one disfigurement; now Paul touches on another trouble-spot, the uncontrolled abandon to spiritual ecstasy, implied in the verb "you were led [astray]" (v. 2). The feature of a trancelike state that characterized the Corinthians' former pagan life (see Gal. 4:3, 8, 9) was carried over into their worship services. He recalls their submission to "idols"—"dumb" not in the sense of making no sound, but rather "dead" and so "unable to help," "powerless" (as in Ps. 115:4–8; Habak. 2:18, 19). Probably the allusion is to the worship of Apollo who was regarded as "seizing" his devotees and inducing in them a frenzied trance like the Sibyl of Cumae (cf. Vergil, *Aeneid,* 6). As Paul would describe it, the devotee was seized, overcome, and "violated" by a demonic power. But this could never be so when the "Lord" (*kyrios*) is Jesus, whatever may have happened in hellenistic ecstatic cults. Paul suggests two reasons for this.

First, the presence of the Holy Spirit who inspires the credal utterance "Jesus is Lord" never "takes over" a person in a way comparable with demonic seizure and possession. (The verb "led" in Gal. 5:18 and presumably Rom. 8:14 must be given a connotation *in bonam partem,* in spite of Käsemann's plea to the contrary.)[3] Paul has already clarified the distinction between Greco-Roman cult practices and the Christian gathering for worship (1 Cor. 10:19–22). Based on his theological ground, Paul's distinctive claim as a Christian lies in his confidence that Christian worship is offered both in the name of and directly to the living Christ. The risen Christ stands in direct opposition to lifeless deities, and to affirm "Jesus is Lord" is to range oneself over against the cultic gods and goddesses of contemporary society. They may claim to be invoked as "lord" (*kyrios*) and "god" (*theos*), but Paul is adamant: "*For us* there is but one God, the Father . . . and there is but one Lord, Jesus Christ" (1 Cor. 8:6).

The other reason that what the Corinthians were doing in the assembly savored more of pagan than of Christian worship is shown in the way Paul will develop his teaching. He insists that "the spirits of the prophets are subject to the control of the prophets. For God is not a God of disorder but of peace. . . . everything should be done in a fitting and orderly way" (1 Cor. 14:32, 33, 40). This insistence sets a boundary line beyond which the authentic expression of worship cannot stray. The Holy Spirit inspires no frenzied outbursts, such as the blasphemous cry "Jesus be damned"—a curse formula that must have sounded as offensive to Paul as it does to us—and his presence is found when "the lordship of Christ"—itself a sure token that he is alive from the dead and has come to greet his people who assemble in his name (Rom. 14:9)—is acknowledged by submission to his authority.

Kyrios is the title of authority, and has been suggestively placed in a context of the church at worship[4] (Rom. 10:9, 10; Phil. 2:11; Rom. 14:11). As Christians invoke this name, they place their lives under the unshared control of the exalted Lord, and by "confession" they express their willing obedience to his power and direction in their lives.

To make this earliest of all the New Testament credal affirmations, recalling a person's baptismal allegiance, is to pass under the authority of that name and to put oneself not on the side of the world (whether Jewish, which regarded Jesus' death as *ḥērem,* under the curse of Deut. 21:23, or pagan, which led its worshipers into unrestrained, excitable blasphemy, or apostate, which found a convenient way of renouncing Christ when tested)[5] but on the side of "the Lord." The Spirit leads believers to acknowledge that Jesus is the sole authority and the inspirer of authentic Christian praise. "Jesus is Lord" is the confession by which the church lives.

THE CHURCH SERVES BY THE POWER OF THE SPIRIT

Paul has clearly established one central point, a "fundamental proposition," as Barrett calls it.[6] "The Holy Spirit makes us receptive to Jesus"; so Eduard Schweizer puts it.[7] Within the orbit of that relationship in which the gift of the Spirit initiates the Christian life and experience (see Gal. 5:25: "since *we are made alive by the Spirit.* . .") and by which the Christian's identity is known (Rom. 8:9, 14, 16), the gifts of the Spirit are received and exercised. The initial gift of the Spirit, for Paul, is unique and singular: it is the awareness of belonging to Christ and becoming part of the divine family of faith. This initiatory experience is spoken of in 12:13 as a "baptism by the one Spirit" into the one family of God whose hallmark is a life in union with the risen Christ, the firstborn of the dead and the eldest son in the family (Col. 1:18; Rom. 8:29). The emphasis falls on a unitary experience incorporating saving faith, or "the hearing that leads to faith" (Gal. 3:2) when the Spirit is received; baptismal allegiance in which the lordship of Christ is openly confessed (Rom. 10:9, 10); and a "religious experience" of filial adoption whose characteristic feature is a calling on God as 'abbā, "dear Father" (Rom. 8:15–17; Gal. 4:4–6), as believers take their place in a new community.

At 1 Corinthians 12:4–10 Paul's thought reaches out to include the consequences of this incorporative act and initial experience. The gift of the Spirit may be one; the gifts of the Spirit are diverse and manifold. The Spirit is one, to be sure, as the fountainhead of the blessings that flow through his agency (as v. 11 will conclude); but the Spirit acts within the structure that can only be described as trinitarian or at least triadic. The "arrangement" is seen in verses 4–6:

The same Spirit . . . yet different kinds of *charismata*
The same Lord (Jesus Christ) . . . yet different kinds of service
  (*diakoniai*)
The same God (the Father) . . . yet different kinds of operations
  (*energēmata*)

It would be wrong to distinguish these "gifts" too sharply. "Gifts, service and working are not distinct categories," comments F. F. Bruce,[8] whereas Arnold Bittlinger wants to see some distinctions.[9] *Charismata* are those ways in which divine grace (*charis*) becomes concrete; *diakoniai* are ministries in which the gifts become real in practice; and the last term suggests outworking with definite effects. What Paul seems intent on stressing is the manifold variety of such gifts that proceed indiscriminately from the several members of the Christian godhead. The key term is "distributions" (*diaireseis*), an idea that goes back to 1 Corinthians 1:7 where Paul acknowledges the giftedness of his readers. The object of such dispersals is the "gifts-in-grace," God's "birthday present" (as *charisma* means in modern Greek) to his children. These *charismata* range over a wide area, numbering around twenty in the New Testament literature.

We should notice the nine gifts Paul itemizes here. F. F. Bruce suggests they rank in descending order of value—in Paul's judgment. Other commentators wish to set them in neatly tabulated categories:

1. Gifts on the intellectual level: words of wisdom and knowledge;
2. Gifts on a plane distinct from the mind: faith, healings, miraculous powers, prophecy, discerning of spirits;
3. Gifts transcending the mind: tongues, interpretation of tongues.

J. W. MacGorman offers a fourfold division:[10]

1. The gifts of intelligible utterance: wisdom, knowledge, and prophecy;
2. The gifts of power: faith, healings, and workings of miracles;
3. The gift of spiritual discernment;
4. The gifts of ecstatic utterance: glossolalia and its interpretation.

Perhaps a more simple arrangement is preferred, following William Baird.[11] We may distinguish:

1. Gifts that are pedagogical, namely, utterances of wisdom and knowledge;
2. Gifts that relate to supernatural power: faith, miracle working, healings;
3. Gifts of special communication: prophecy, the ability to discern spirits (i.e., in the assessment of prophecies), the gift of tongues, and interpretation.

We hope to show that this way of describing the charismatic gifts is borne out by what Paul says in later discussion (notably in 1 Cor. 14).

Some comments are now needed to set this series of grace-gifts in its context.

First, Paul remarks at the outset on the inclusive scope of these gifts. We notice the terms that run like a thread throughout this section: "in all men" (= persons; v. 6); "to each man" (v. 7, but the Greek does not have this sexist language); "all these" gifts are bestowed on the church without discrimination as to gender, social station, ethical maturity, or native endowments. Clearly Paul has his eye on the factious spirit that prevailed at Corinth, splitting the church into cliques and party divisions. His line of reasoning is calculated to emphasize the importance of the individual within the wider company of the church. Yet he draws back from commending those Corinthians who were gifted with the more exotic *charismata* and therefore thought they could despise their fellow believers. Hence the climax comes in verse 12: there is one body of which all, without exception, form a vital part.

Second, while all Christians have some gift, not all have the same gift. The repeated term *diaireseis* (vv. 4–6) is possibly chosen as a double entendre in Paul's vocabulary. He is facing a church rent into many subgroups (see 11:18, 19: "there are cleavages of opinion among you"; *haireseis*) on the basis of social standing, spiritual elitism, and cultural diversity, with the most serious fault their theological differences over baptism (1:11–17) and claims to private *gnōsis* (8:1). Yet he selects the strong Greek word *diaireseis,* which comes from *di-hairein* meaning to tear apart, to split, to dismember. Is Paul deliberately being provocative? There are divisions in your midst, he reports, yet God distributes his many gifts to you nonetheless. Your false understanding of baptism (1:13) means that Christ is being parcelled out; yet God reverses this tendency by giving to you from one common, indivisible source a rich variety of his gifts.

Third, the nine *charismata,* "the concrete realization of divine grace," are clearly only a sample listing. "The list is not intended to be exhaustive" (Bruce);[12] and the series should not be regarded as mandatory, since not all the gifts may be present at the same time and place. Nor should Paul's enumeration be regarded as "closed" since we must allow—on the basis of verse 11—the sovereign Spirit to fashion new gifts for fresh occasions and special needs as they will arise in the life and service of the church that, like a living organism, continues to grow and develop.

Finally, the choice Paul makes of these gifts is determined by the situation at Corinth. "Wisdom" and "knowledge" were clearly watchwords among the people there, especially as the church lay under the spell of an incipient Gnosticism that set great store by these qualities. Already Paul has contrasted two types of wisdom (*sophia*), both speculative and saving, in 1 Corinthians 2:6–13, and already he has exposed the dangers inherent in a false knowledge (*gnōsis,* in 8:1, 7, 11). He now rescues both terms from the Corinthian pneumatics and gives them a fresh stamp.[13] For Paul, says E. Earle Ellis,[14] the criterion that certifies the valid use of the prophetic gifts of wisdom and knowledge is a "true perception and manifestation of the mind of Christ," citing 1 Corinthians 2:16. Such understanding lies over against human dialectics (3:20), which in turn produce only "fleshly wisdom," a wisdom of "this age" (1:20; 3:18f.; cf. 2 Cor. 1:12) and under the influence of demonic powers. The link then is with 12:3 and its denial of those who claim to be led by "spirit" into blasphemous utterance. On the contrary, the Christian teacher, exercising a truly pneumatic gift, will function in a way that exalts the lordship of Christ as a faithful steward of the divine mysteries (1 Cor. 4:1) and with particular reference to owning Christ as Lord. (A good illustration is seen in *Didache* 11.)

The second group of *charismata* relates to gifts of supernatural endowment: "faith," which is not the saving faith that is true of all believers but a special endowment for special service (13:2). It is "faith" that works miracles, akin to the gifts of "healings" and the performing of "mighty works" (*dynameis*) such as those wrought by Jesus in his messianic capacity and the apostles in his name (Mark 6:2; cf. 6:5; Acts 2:22, 43). The "faith" that is so signally exercised may well be the imparting of confident expectation to the sick so that *they* receive the gift of healing (so Bittlinger);[15] and the plural of "healing" may suggest both spiritual renewal and physical recovery.

The final section covers gifts related to communication. First is "prophecy," which is more amply defined in chapter 14, its essence in verse 3: "everyone who prophesies speaks to men for their strengthening, encouragement and comfort," though some (like Bruce) think more of the foretelling aspect seen in the case of Agabus (Acts 11:28; 21:10f.) or Philip's daughters (Acts 21:9). Since this latter gift was not subject to investigation (though Paul did not treat it as compelling in its authority) it is better to see "prophecy" as a charismatic gift of "exhortatory preaching" (*paraklēsis*) in the context of a "ministry of pastoral teaching and instruction" serving to upbuild the community, as David Hill describes it.[16] Then we can relate it to the "distinguishing of spirits," since "prophecy" is subject to evaluation and assessment by other prophets, both male (14:29f.) and presumably female (11:5). "Tongues" suggest ecstatic speech, called in 13:1 "the tongues of angels," which obviously need "interpretation" (*hermeneia*) if the hearer is to be edified by what is spoken in the assembly (14:13–19). These matters will be fully considered later.

THE CHURCH THRIVES IN FELLOWSHIP

The punch line of Paul's opening statement comes in 12:11: "All these [*charismata*] are the work of one and the same Spirit, and he gives them to each man [= person], *just as he determines*." The final phrase, "as he pleases," suggests an acknowledgment of divine sovereignty and control. "The gift has the character of free grace," comments Conzelmann. But such bestowal (or withholding) is not capricious or accidental. A rationale has already been given at verse 7: all the charismatic gifts are to serve "the common good" and should be for the growth of the entire congregation in mutual understanding of God's will, which is *koinōnia*. The stress on unity ("one Spirit") points back to this principle, and looks ahead to Paul's powerful baptismal reminder in verses 12 and 13, where he emphasizes the "one body" motif.

Here is the most illuminating word on the *charismata*. They act as a bridge between "one Spirit" and "one body," and proceed as the unfettered gift of the one source intended to enrich and develop the members of the body. Their purpose is therefore functional— to promote the God-given unity of the church, made up of many parts—and also confirmatory—thereby acting in a double way, says Barrett, [17] in rebuking any Christian who is tempted to boast as well as in encouraging any Christian who feels a sense of deprivation and inferiority. Since the Spirit gives or withholds, both attitudes are mistaken. And since the Spirit is one, unity is of the essence of the church's life.

The only thing that really unites people, said Augustine, is a common desire for the same ends. The charismatic Spirit offers gifts and instills such a desire precisely for that reason (14:1).

Translation

12–14   Just as the body is one but has many parts, and all the *parts*ᵃ of the one body, though they are many, are one body, so it is also with *the Messiah*.ᵇ For in one Spirit we were all baptized into one body, whether we were Jews or Hellenes, slaves or free; and we were all given one Spirit as *outpoured* (on us).ᶜ The body is not one part but many.

15–27   If the *foot*ᵈ says, "Because I am not a hand I do not belong to the body," does it *for that reason*ᵉ not belong to the body? If the *ear*ᵈ says, "Because I am not an eye, I do not belong to the body," does it *for that reason*ᵉ not belong to the body?

If the whole body were an eye, where would the hearing be? If the whole body were hearing, where would the sense of smell be? *As it is,*ᵍ God has placed the parts, each one of them, in the body, just *as he chose.*ᶠ

If they were all one part, where would the body be? *As it is,*ᵍ there are many parts, but one body. The eye cannot say to the hand, "I do not need you," nor again the head to the feet, "I do not need you." No, much rather, the parts of the body which *seem to be weaker*ʰ are necessary, and we clothe with greater honor the parts of the body which we think less honorable. Our unseemly parts are made more seemly, whereas our seemly parts do not need anything. But God has put the body together, giving greater honor to the part which lacks it, that there may be no division in the body, but that the parts may have the same concern for one another. If one part suffers, all the parts suffer with it. If one part is praised, all the parts rejoice with it. You are the body of Christ, and individually parts of it.

28–31   These then God has placed in the church. First, apostles; secondly, prophets; thirdly, teachers; then mighty works, then spiritual gifts of healings, supports, administrative gifts, different kinds of tongues.ⁱ Are all apostles?ʲ Are all prophets? Are all teachers? Do all (perform) mighty works? Do all (have) spiritual gifts of healings? Do all speak in tongues? Do all interpret?

You are seeking then the "greatest gifts," are you?ᵏ Well, I intend to show you a still better way.

Points to Ponder

a. "Parts" renders μέλη, which can also mean "members" in a double sense: bodily organs or limbs, and "church members" (12:27).

b. ὁ Χριστός: The article suggests the technical sense of the noun, "the Christ."

c. ἐποτίσθημεν, lit. "we were saturated" in one Spirit. A reference to baptism is suggested (see R. P. Martin, *The Worship of God* [1982], 183).

d. Note the play on words: πούς (foot), οὖς (ear).

e. παρὰ τοῦτο, "for that reason."

f. καθὼς ἠθέλησεν matches v. 11, καθὼς βούλεται.

g. A good example of νῦν/νυνὶ = "as it is," a logical sense, not temporal. Refer to 13:13.

h. Who are these church members "who deem [themselves] to be weaker"? See E. Best, *One Body in Christ* (1955), 102. A sociological interpretation is given by G. Theissen, *The Social Setting of Pauline Christianity* (ET 1982), 56, 72, citing 1 Cor. 4:9–13.

i. Why does the NIV add "finally," do you think? Note that the latest revision of the NIV drops the adverb. See G. D. Fee, "Tongues—Least of the Gifts? Some Exegetical Observations on 1 Cor. 12–14," *Pneuma* 2 (1980):3.

j. The Greek μὴ expects the answer "No" in each case; vv. 29, 30.

k. G. Iber (accepted by Bittlinger, *Gifts and Graces,* 73) takes this as indicative, not imperative (NIV). I agree but also take it as a question. μείζονα could be comparative (greater). If so, what is the meaning?

CHAPTER TWO

BODY LIFE

INTRODUCTION

Paul's discussion in 1 Corinthians 12:1–11 has its center in verse 7: "to each person the revelation of the Spirit is given for the common good." The commentators Robertson and Plummer suggest Paul's interest in 12:8–10 is to focus on the individualizing scope of the Spirit's gifts; hence the repeated "to each," "to one person," "to another" (vv. 7a, 8–10). At verse 12 he moves into an exposition of what is implied in the second half of verse 7, "for the common good."

Whether or not this is too schematic an arrangement, it remains that 12:12–31 is devoted to enforcing the corporate nature both of the church's life and the use of the *charismata*.

We should remind ourselves of the chief issue at stake. James Denney put it in a memorable sentence:[1] "the Church of Christ was for them"—the Corinthians—"a stage on which they aspired to be conspicuous figures." This trait became evident in their desire for "spiritual gifts"; and Paul has had to recall them to the way the Spirit acts sovereignly in his gifts (12:11) and the purpose for which the *charismata* are supplied. It is "for the common good," a phrase that means literally "with a view to what is for the best" (*pros to sympheron*; see 1 Cor. 6:12; 10:23). As Conzelmann remarks, this purpose is an aspect of *oikodomē*, "upbuilding," which in turn focuses attention on the well-being and maturity of the entire community, not the individual (14:12).

Yet Paul is realistic enough to know that the whole is made up of many parts, as verse 12 states. And he is led into the discussion of "the body" by two opposing tendencies prevailing at Corinth. We will now consider these.

THE CORINTHIANS' ATTITUDES

The key phrase comes in verse 25: "that there should be no division in the body, but that the parts (*or* members) may harmoniously provide for each other" (Conzelmann's wording). The antecedent of this summary conclusion takes us right to the heart of Paul's theological thinking: "God has fitted the body together" in such a way that the antidote to the Corinthians' divisiveness and party grouping (1:10, 11; 11:18 speak of their *schismata*) has already been given. And that wording takes us back to 12:12 and 13.

But the church members at Corinth were acting in several ways that ignored or contradicted what the apostle regarded as basic understanding of the nature of the church. They had overlooked what the first part of his discussion had clearly stated: all Christians have some gift of the Spirit, but not all have the same gift. The variety in grace is as rich and manifold as the variety in nature. Moreover, the Spirit reserves the right to give or withhold, so no one should be envious of another. By the same token a person should not feel slighted or passed over because he or she does not enjoy the more spectacular gifts.

These two attitudes evidently were much in prominence. So Paul in elaborating the body metaphor (introduced at vv. 12, 13) puts into the mouth of different organs of the human body sentiments, complaints, and claims that assert what the Corinthian readers were saying. To be sure, the cause of both ill-fated, distempered remarks may well be the same, as Conzelmann argues. Both traits reflect "the practice of individuals' dissociating themselves from the 'body.'" But it does seem that the same pulling apart from the church's true life and existence took on two quite distinct forms.

(a) There were those who suffered from an *inferiority complex,* feeling they could never aspire to the more flamboyant and "showy" gifts of service. As a result they demeaned themselves and took on what J. Weiss calls an "all too humble self-assessment." We hear them speak in the complaint of the foot, "Because I am not a hand, I do not belong to the body," or in the ear's lament, "Because I am not an eye, I do not belong to the body" (vv. 15, 16; Weiss also observes the assonance of these two anatomical members, *pous,* foot; *ous,* ear). Put into modern idiom, the bodily "member" becomes the church "member" who is often heard sadly to confess: "I'm nothing of value; I'm a nobody," with the implied self-justification, "Don't expect a lot from me; don't ask me to take on responsibility; don't call on me to serve, I haven't the gift."

(b) At the other extreme were those prominent Christians in the assembly who claimed a full share of the Spirit's largesse, turning this boastful claim into a *superiority complex,* as verse 21 represents them saying. Imagining that because they *did* have great gifts much in demand, they aspired to be important figures in their own right. The tendency was that they started to look down on others and despise them. Their voice is heard in what the eye would say to the hand, "I don't need you!" or in the head disclaiming any connection with the feet, "I don't need you!" Such dialogue between the anatomical organs picks up a conversation between eye and head, two parts of the body generally recognized as the most prominent members. But for these admittedly important organs to dissociate themselves from "hand" and "feet" (these two parts do go together) is patently "absurd" (Conzelmann). When applied to the human members of the body of Christ, the analogy is just as convincing. Such an exalted opinion needs deflating, and the complementary bringing together of the body into "harmony" and "unity" is Paul's antidote.

In fact, Paul's solution to these twin grievous errors at Corinth is the same in both instances. He stresses the unity of the church and the interdependence of the members, with a final recall that not everyone functions in the same way. His choice of illustration is one all his readers, ancient and modern, could appreciate, since we are all familiar with it: it is the human body. In fact, "body" (*sōma*) for Paul is a key concept in his theology, as recent studies have shown, and it has the further merit of being a universal, transcultural association. All human beings recognize the language of the body, and both the ideas of physicality and personhood ("body" meaning "self"-identity, as in the expression "every*body*" = every*one*) are to the fore in Pauline anthropology and his teaching on "Christ and the church."

PAUL'S USE OF THE BODY ANALOGY

Beginning with verse 12, Paul's discussion is "dominated by the figure of the body as an organism" (Conzelmann), as he compares the church to a human body. In the best-known example of this illustration, Menenius Agrippa, a Roman consul in 503 B.C., had appeased the plebs who threatened to destroy the city life by secession by his telling the parable of the "Belly and the Limbs." The thrust of the tale is that plebeian interests were the same as those of the patricians—since all Romans belonged to the same body politic—and therefore they should not go on strike.

> There was a day when the human body was not as harmoniously ordered as it is today. Every member of the body had its own will and its own language. The other members became angry that they had to concern themselves with the need of the stomach, and provide it with everything. The stomach just remained at the centre of all this satisfied with all that was brought to it. The members made this decision: the hands would not supply any food to the mouth—the mouth would not receive any food nor would the teeth chew. Consequently during this time in which they starved the stomach all the parts of the body became weak and feeble. Then they realized that the role of the stomach was not to be despised as a passive one. Just as he was being nourished, he was passing on strength in return. (Livy, *Urb. Cond.* 2.32; cf. 3.54)

The Stoics took up this notion of interdependence both politically and philosophically. Their watchword was "sympathy" (*sympatheia*), that is, fellow-feeling that unites members of the community. The latter idea goes back to Plato:

> When one of us has a wounded finger, the body and soul of the person and their inter-relationship are affected, we say *the man* feels pain in his finger. Even so with every other part of the body—when one part suffers there is pain, and there is joy when one part is restored to health. (*Rep.* 462 C–D)

In the hands of Seneca (*Ep.* 95.52: "we are members of a great body" whose hallmark is that it is one, embracing human and divine) and Epictetus (*Diss.* 2.10.3f.) the philosophical idea that God and man are one was extended to include the cosmic: "You are a citizen of the world and a part (*meros*) of it . . . [one should act] as the foot or hand which, if they had the faculty of reason and understood the constitution of nature, [they] would never exercise choice or desire in any other way but by reference to the whole."

Two uses of the body idea were evidently current in Paul's day: (*i*) the world or society formed a compact unit, and no part could properly act as though it alone existed and counted; (*ii*) when one section suffers, all are affected, just as the disease or weakness of one bodily organ is felt through the entire human frame (see Josephus, *Jewish War* 4.406, for this observation also).

Paul may well be indebted to these popular ideas, and it is striking that he does introduce the element of pain into the body analogy (at 12:26)—a common Stoic principle. But two extra dimensions to this man's mind need to be added.

First, Paul's Jewish upbringing and intellectual training would no doubt have prepared and equipped him for making use of the idea that a unitary figure can contain within it the associations of a body. The remnant in Israel; the I-figure who speaks in the Psalms; the "servant" in Isaiah 40–55; and the "son of man" in Daniel's apocalyptic vision (7:13–27)—all these diverse strands of Jewish thought come together in the conviction that "one" voice may act and speak for a representative group, and that what looks to be a singular concept (body) has the flexibility to fan out to embrace many parts.

Second, we should not underrate the continuing effect on Paul's theology of his conversion experience as that became understood. Granted that he never gives the dramatic details of the Damascus road encounter in so many words as we have in the Acts record, it still is remarkable how Luke's account (Acts 9:4, 5) seems to be echoed in Paul's later teaching of "sinning against Christ" (1 Cor. 8:12). John A. T. Robinson[2] and more recently Seyoon Kim[3] have argued that Paul's conversion involved the association of the heavenly Lord with his people whom as a Pharisee he was persecuting. Out of this vivid realization, "I am Jesus whom you are persecuting," came Paul's theological construct of the church as Christ's body or person.

If there is substance in these two elements in the background of Paul's thought on the church, it will help us to decide what kind of identity is meant in our passage (12:12, 13). A slightly expanded rendering would be:

> The body is one, though it is composed of many parts, and though all its parts are many, they form one body. So it is with [the] Christ. For we were all baptized in one Spirit into one body—whether Jews or Hellenes, slaves or free persons—and we were all imbued with one Spirit.

The first difficulty is eased when we see how Paul has taken "two steps in one," as C. K. Barrett says. From his initial statement that the one body has nevertheless several parts, we would expect him to conclude: so it is with *the church*. Instead, he jumps on to equate "church" and the Messiah as a single entity. This is best explained in the analogy of the head-and-the-members joined as a unitary concept; and there is a line of interpreters from Augustine, Aquinas, and Calvin to modern commentators that sees how Paul regards Christ and his people as forming one entity, the whole Christ (*totus Christus*). Some writers, such as Aquinas and Lietzmann, speak of a mystical union joining Christ and the church. But this is a term of doubtful meaning in this context. A better suggestion is the Hebraic idea of "corporate oneness," so that Christ and his people form a total, inclusive person. Together they are "one body," which the later letters in the Pauline corpus will interpret in terms of Christ the head and the church as his members, thus moving the discussion forward from here and Romans 12:4–8 (see Col. 1:18; 2:19; Eph. 1:22; 4:15; 5:23). In our text the thought is simpler, but with a practical intent as it concentrates on the interrelatedness of the many members, united in the interest of the well-being of the whole.

Paul's answer to the fragmented character of the Corinthian church is to assert the inextricable unity of the body, based on its christological model ("one Christ" = one body). A second rationale and plea for unity comes in verse 13, in which he argues on the basis of Christian experience. It was by "one Spirit" that all were initiated into the one body, and this shared experience, actualized in baptism and incorporation, cancels out even the inveterate distinctions that kept people apart in the ancient world. From this "one baptism"—best regarded as described under two metaphors ("baptized" in the water rite and "saturated" [*epotisthēmen*][4] by the Spirit in the same initiatory experience)—Paul extrapolates that barriers of race, culture, and social status are done away in an "eschatological abrogation," that is, in Christ and in the new age of eschatological salvation they no longer exist. This means that "in the church" that is part of God's new order these idealized conditions take on reality as baptism provides the gateway to the communal life-in-Christ.

Thus, before further developing his body analogy, Paul has set his position on a firm theological base. "One Christ" postulates "one body," yet there is diversity within the unity. But diversity is not conflict. "One Spirit" is the agent of initiation, just as in baptism the new converts, drawn from a wide spectrum of contemporary life, find in a common experience that which confirms their place in a new society in which cultural disharmonies, class rivalries, and social disabilities are transcended in a new status. "Jews," "Hellenes," "slaves," "free persons" all remain in the empirical world (1 Cor. 7:17–24); but in Christ's fellowship they are only name tags, not isolating, discriminating terms (Gal. 3:28, 29).

Paul is now ready, with this argument clearly laid, to address his major theme. The thesis is set out (in the long section of vv. 14–26) that unity is not contradicted by diversity, for diversity is not incompatible with his initial emphasis on the body's oneness. He offers four statements to enforce his position.

(a) *Every Christian is a necessary member of the community* (vv. 14–16). This is the first application of the analogy of the "one body" and its "many members." The preceding verses accentuate the "oneness"; with verse 14 Paul highlights the "many" in the interest of showing how the manifold variety of the body's parts does not invalidate—but rather illustrates—the interdependence that binds the parts of the body together.

As we have seen, there are anticipations of this analogy in Stoic thought and teaching. Paul's treatment, however, is far more insistent on the impossibility of one bodily organ becoming amputated from the rest of the whole body—even if that organ, now personified, wanted to cut itself off. And certainly—and this is the apostle's point driven home in the face of the Corinthians' predicament of mutual rivalries and jealousies (see 1 Cor. 3:3)—it is foolish for one member (the foot or the ear) to want to detach itself from the corporate whole because it is not some other member. Every part of the human body is a necessary part in the harmonious functioning of the whole.

The application of this analogy to the church at Corinth is not easy to pinpoint. Presumably the complaint voiced by the foot or the ear is not that such members feel aggrieved because they are not the only members of the body. So the complaining Corinthians were not expressing disappointment that they did not possess *all* the *charismata* (so Lietzmann). The notion is rather one of envy and dissatisfaction. The case is that of a Christian who had one charism and yet is denied access to what others in the community felt were the more important gifts (evidently glossolalia). He then begins to doubt his own standing as a believer, and regards himself as cut off from the church. Paul vigorously denies this conclusion and has a pastoral word of encouragement for such an individual. His twice-repeated expression (*para touto*; vv. 15, 16) is intended exactly to refute this false deduction. Just to say "I do not have this gift, so I do not belong to the body" alters nothing. The member does not *for that reason* cease to belong. That is Paul's word of consolation, but it is equally a word of rebuke, challenging the resentment of the rejected members who evidently were taking to heart what was said about them at Corinth, namely, that they were "less honorable" (v. 23). Paul calls on them to refuse that demeaning title and to see their true place in the Christian community. Every Christian *belongs*: that would be the thrust of Paul's counterreply to the lament in verses 14–16.

(b) *Every Christian needs the help of every other Christian* (vv. 17–22). Perhaps Paul is continuing here to reassure the "weaker" members. He offers two reasons to set his encouragement on a firm base. First, in the human body variety is not only desirable, it is necessary. To imagine a body that consisted only of a gigantic eye or a colossal ear is to contemplate a monstrosity, an *ektrōma* (1 Cor. 15:8) in one of its several meanings. Whatever such a "monster" would be, it would not function as the human body functions because other senses—of hearing in the one case, or smell in the other—would be missing. Each bodily organ works in conjunction with the others, and indeed if it wanted to exist on its own, it would not—and could not—exist in the body (v. 19). Conversely, if it fails to do its job, the whole body feels the effect of the breakdown, a point mentioned in Plato, as we saw earlier, and to which Paul will return in verse 26.

Second, God has arranged the organs of the body, every one of them, in a way that he chose (v. 18, a phrase that goes back to 12:11, "just as he determined"). E. Käsemann[5] neatly sums up the strength of Paul's argument that moves on now (at v. 21) to address the arrogant members who profess to have no need of their fellow believers:

> No one, according to I Cor. 12.21, may say to his brother, "I have no need of you." Over them all stands the sign *kathōs bouletai* or *ēthelēsen* (I Cor. 12.11, 18); this expresses the sovereignty of the divine grace and omnipotence, which is both liberal and liberating, which puts an end to worry and envy by giving individually to every man. No one goes away empty, but no one has too much.

The effective answer to the Corinthians' pride, shown in their disdaining of brethren who did not have the more exuberant "gifts of grace," comes finally in Paul's reminder that the so-called "weaker members" of the human body are indispensable (vv. 21, 22). The attitude found in these verses—the eye and the head claiming "I have no need of" the hand and the feet—is confirmed by a stylistic change in Paul's writing. Whereas the complaining foot and ear speak only to themselves, the more boastful members in verse 21 address their remarks directly to the members they look down on; and their condescending manner is both attitudinal and actual: the eye and the head are elevated above the other members in the human frame.

Paul will have none of this. He knows "bodily members that are accounted weaker," such as delicate organs, are all the more necessary to the body's proper functioning. It is strange that he should have cast the eye in the role of a speaker in verse 21, since the eye is a delicate organ yet is made to speak as a "stronger" member claiming independence. It is easier to identify the remaining two adjectives, as we shall observe. Perhaps the more feeble members (v. 22) are introduced to rebuke their counterparts. Paul is attacking those haughty Corinthians who not only imagined themselves enjoying an independent status in the community ("I have no need of" others) but actually treated as nonmembers of the church those who did not aspire to the more spectacular gifts. And Paul's point is that, according to his standards, in the life-in-Christ to which all are introduced by baptism and the gift of the Spirit, there is interrelationship and reciprocal dependence that makes a "solo performance" type of Christian living and service unthinkable (Rom. 14:7; cf. Eph. 4:25b). Both the resentment of the weak and the pride of the strong are answered by this apostolic insistence on "many parts, but one body" (v. 20).

(c) *Every Christian is complemented by others* (vv. 23–25). Paul is continuing to explain the nature of church life under the figure of a body. Although he has made the equation "the church = the [body of] Christ" (v. 12) and will repeat this equivalence of terms in 12:27, it seems clear that the language is metaphorical and illustrative. Attempts to read into his use of the "body" a literal identity and so a pedantic correspondence of "members" with the Corinthian situation quickly break down. "We must not try to fit every detail into the life of the Church in Corinth," E. Best wisely cautions.[6] Yet points of similarity remain, since Paul is obviously exploiting the double meaning found in the Greek *melos,* which stands for both a bodily "member" and a "member" of the church.

This paragraph emphasizes how particular respect should be shown to those members of the community who appear to be less important than the rest. The criterion adopted by the Corinthians themselves was presumably the possession of the more "flowery" charismatic gifts. These gifts were taken to be tokens of a person's importance in the eyes of God. And that reference to a divine endowment given to some but withheld from others is why Paul meets the Corinthian pneumatics on their own ground.

His discussion begins with the common recognition that some parts of the human torso are less attractive than others. The adjectives are "less honorable" (*atimotera;* v. 23) and "[more] unpresentable" (NIV), "unseemly" (Barrett, Conzelmann), "indecorous" (Moffatt). Perhaps a stronger translation is called for: the root is "shame," so more "shameful," bordering on "indecent," is suggested (cf. Rom. 1:27). A sexual reference seems implied in view of other occurrences of the word (Rev. 3:18; 16:15; cf. 1 Cor. 7:36), though not exclusively so (1 Cor. 13:5). On balance, however, the "uncomely parts" (*aschēmona*) seem to describe the sexual organs, as *atimotera* refer to the gastric organs, notably the stomach. Paul reflects local custom in remarking that those parts of the torso whose functions we conceal we clothe with honor—an allusion possibly to Genesis 3:7, 10, 21—and those parts we treat as "private" and do not expose, we accord a special modesty. So far the analogy holds.

The difficulty comes in trying to relate these descriptive remarks to church members. Are they, as Best suggests, members who work only in the background and attract no attention? Or is the point of connection the fact that some members are drawn from a lower social stratum than others, and so are of humbler origin (1 Cor. 1:26; 11:22)? Or is Paul's point simply that *all* parts of the body are needful for a healthy construction and so *all* Christians should be welcomed as having a role to play in the body life? This last idea seems plausible.

The next difficulty lies in Paul's introduction of a providential ordering (v. 24). The Stoics would argue from "what is fitting" and in accordance with "nature" (*physis*). Paul brings in God as the one who not only arranges the parts of the body (v. 18), but now (v. 24) has "put the body together" in a union that has no room for "divisions" (*schismata*, a reference back to 1 Cor. 1:10; 11:18, which mention the party groups and social distinctions within the Corinthian assembly). This "compounding" (a Stoic term for the fusing of elements in the natural order) is achieved by God (for Paul) by giving greater honor to the parts of the body that lack it. The question is posed, How does God do that? Ernest Best is one of the few commentators to raise the point; his answer is that God does it through his people, noting that at verse 23 Paul suddenly brings onto the scene a human evaluation: the parts *we think* are less honorable. The Pauline inference would be that *we* are to reckon others worthy of honor and so avoid the creating of divisions that were so ruinous to the fellowship at Corinth.

So the body, both human and ecclesial, is meant to be "adorned" and made beautiful. Paul here seems to be talking of attractiveness and appeal. Members that need little cosmetic enhancement (face, legs) can only show their best if they are complemented by other parts of the body that need clothing and "special treatment" (v. 24). Then even those ungainly parts set off the excellence of the more alluring parts. The body is meant to appear as one, as well as to function without discord; and this is now applied to the "body of Christ" in its nuptial union with the Lord (for the "bridal dignity" of the church, cf. Eph. 5:26, 27; Rev. 19:7, 8).

(d) *Every Christian is involved with other Christians* (vv. 25, 26). From the Stoics Paul may have learned of "sympathy," the fellow-feeling that unites the cosmos and humankind in suffering and pain. Plato—as we noted—remarked that when a finger is hurt, the whole bodily unity (*koinōnia*) suffers with it . . . and so we say that the man has a pain in his finger. Josephus has the same thought: "if one member of the body is sick and enflamed . . . the other members cannot recuperate, for they share in the illness."

C. K. Barrett does not think the physiological metaphor holds when we reverse it to include not only pain and suffering but being honored and rejoicing. Yet there is a sense in which one organ's well-being profits the entire body and gives a general sense of well-being and overall health. But undoubtedly Paul's thought is more

relevant to the body life of the church. Christians are bound together in a common experience in which the pain and joy of one is
distributed, for woe or weal, through the entire fellowship.

We can perhaps more easily grasp the idea of "fellowship-in-
suffering," since nothing in human experience touches us more
acutely with a sense of compassion (i.e., suffering-with) than the
sight of a neighbor or friend in deep distress. Paul's own pastoral
identity with a person in need or in spiritual danger is a good
example: "Who is weak, and I do not feel weak? Who is led into
sin, and I do not inwardly burn?" he asks rhetorically (2 Cor.
11:29). The corresponding "joy-sharing" is characteristic of Paul,
since by the same token that we are united in suffering he can
conclude that we are honored in the esteem that comes to one
member. The theological background of this thought, admittedly
not developed here, is that as Christ was honored in his resurrection and exaltation, we too shall share in that glory (Rom. 8:17,
30; cf. 2 Tim. 2:12).

Whether in pain or prosperity, what binds Christians together
is the "concern" that they are to have for one another. We have
already drawn attention to this word, rendered "concern," "anxiety," in the light of Paul's pastoral regard (2 Cor. 11:28). In its
negative connotation Paul can write a warning: don't be anxious
(Phil. 4:6; cf. 1 Cor. 7:32; Matt. 6:34)—for yourself. Here is
perhaps the one exception to that pejorative sense, and he calls on
his readers to be "anxious"—on others' behalf, a different application of the word, to be sure!

Verse 27 is a summary statement, joining together both a descriptive and a declarative statement in a manner typical of Pauline
ethical admonitions: become what you already are. "You are the
body of Christ" is the basic datum, ensured by God's design and
the baptismal initiation (12:13). Now, Paul concludes, prove
yourselves to be "each one of you a part of it" (ek merous is best taken
in this sense, as Weiss translates: "each for his own part")

MODES OF MINISTRY

The swift oscillation of Paul's agile mind swings over to include a
discussion of how Christ's body functions. The body analogy
stresses functionality as its chief feature. As Eduard Schweizer
remarks:

This usage of the term "body" would open the way for an understanding of the body-of-Christ concept in which the church would be considered as the instrument by which Christ did his continuing service to the world.[7]

This statement assumes that the genitive in the expression "body of Christ" (*sōma Christou*) is one of possession and authority. The church is that segment of human life which belongs to Christ and fulfills its destiny in doing his service. The next question is bound to be raised, however: How does the body act in this way? And what are the types of service the "parts" render to the body? The reply to these questions comes in verses 28–30, introduced by a strong asseveration: "These are the ones God has appointed in the church." First, a numerical sequence of persons (apostles, prophets, teachers) who constitute "the primary Christian ministry," as Barrett calls it. These are followed by a list of gifts, not persons; and this in an unnumbered fashion, which gives the appearance of being quoted in an indefinite, open-ended way. Hence we dispute the insertion of "finally" into the NIV translation (1978) as without a corresponding Greek adverb and as misleading (see above, p. 18).

The setting of these ministries "in the church" has raised a question of whether Paul has in mind the "local" or the "universal" church. The apostle uses both senses of the term *ekklēsia*, but the scales are tipped on the side of the latter by referring back to verse 27: "you are the body of Christ." All agree that this phrase carries the endorsement of the local church as the locus of Christ's presence, authority, and power; the question is whether Paul ever thought of a transcendental dimension of the church, of which the local community was a visible and concrete paradigm. Robert Banks has recently denied this and argues for an exclusive "local" sense of *ekklēsia*.[8] But the prescript of 1 Corinthians (1:2: "the church of God [that is] in Corinth") and a later reference to "the church of God" (15:9) suggest that what Paul had in view was the universal church of which the Corinthian Christians formed a local outgrowth. This conclusion is important in assessing the role of the persons named in 12:28. They would be not a body of local officials in the Corinthian assembly but God's appointment in the worldwide community—of which, naturally, Corinth formed a part. But the ministries listed are those exercised in the various Christian centers, and that suggests an itinerant type of service.

At the head of the list stand "apostles," a term whose basic sense is "ones sent," having been called by the risen Lord and commissioned to proclaim the good news, as Paul had been (1 Cor. 1:17; 9:1; 15:9). Other meanings of the term are attested, such as delegates of the congregation, for example, Epaphroditus (Phil. 2:25); or Paul's agents sent to the churches, as the unnamed men of 2 Corinthians 8:22, 23; or the original charter members of the Jerusalem mother church (Acts 1:21f.). Of particular interest, however, is the way the "original" apostles, including Paul, came to be looked upon as a "closed circle," laying—or being themselves—the foundation on which the universal church rests (Eph. 2:20; 3:5; cf. Rev. 21:14). The reason for the preeminent place accorded "apostles" is well described by C. K. Barrett, who refers to the fundamental study of A. Fridrichsen:

> Their work [says Barrett] did not simply bear witness to the deeds of God in the last days; it was itself part of the eschatological events, and in the Gospel they preached the righteousness of God was manifested (Rom. 1:17).[9]

This point is important in defining (and delineating) the scope of the apostolic office since (*i*) it shows the apostle to be *sui generis* in the way Paul uses the word as a technical expression, namely, "the eschatological person" whose role not only conveys the gospel but is part of its coming to effective expression; (*ii*) it marks off Paul's claim as a "true" apostle from the counterfeit variety (2 Cor. 11:13; 12:12); and (*iii*) it will show how logical is the expected answer to the rhetorical question posed in verse 29: "Are all apostles?" The answer is No, not all Christians may be apostles.

The order of "prophets" (e.g., Agabus in Acts 11:27f.; 21:10) was concerned with the revelation of the divine will for the congregations (e.g., at Antioch, Acts 13:1), a function shared with "teacher" whose business was one of instructing fellow believers "in the meaning and moral implications of the Christian faith" (Barrett, citing Gal. 6:6).

These three offices stand together in Ephesians 4:11 where they are represented as the gift of the exalted Christ, intended to be (*i*) for the training of God's people for works of service, but (*ii*) perhaps more vitally as the "supporting ligament" uniting the head (Christ) with the members (church people) and promoting their growth and progress in love, as each part is equipped to do its work (Eph. 4:16). [10]

After enumerating these persons Paul shifts to a description of gifts and functions, some of which have been alluded to already ("miracles," 12:10; "gifts of healings," 12:9; "tongues," 12:10). The designations that are new on the scene pose problems of their own. Two hard-to-translate Greek words speak of two functions that were evidently in the Corinthian church life: *antilēmpseis* (the verb means to support, help, undertake) and *kybernēseis* (the root word means to steer a ship; cf. Acts 27:11; Rev. 18:17, both nautical references). So "helpers" and "administrators" are so called from the service certain persons fulfilled in the ways indicated. The gifts of "support" and "direction" could be equated with "deacons" and "bishops" respectively, since the deacons (at Philippi in Phil. 1:1; 1 Tim. 3:8–10; *Didache* 15:1, 2; cf. Acts 6:1–7 which speaks of the service of the seven) and the bishops (also at Philippi and Ephesus, 1 Tim. 3:1–7) roughly correspond, it would appear, to these responsibilities. The persons in question minister the church's aid to the needy and preside over church meetings (Rom. 12:8). We should observe, however, that this equivalence is at best a guess, and others, including Phoebe at Cenchraea (Rom. 16:1), are called deacons in a more undefined way. What does seem more certain is that "bishops" and "deacons" exercised a settled vocation in a local congregation over against the peripatetic ministry of "prophets" and "teachers."

As Paul lists the seven categories of service, each with a rhetorical question, he seems to be adopting a descending scale of values (as in 12:8–10); and his questions are so phrased as to expect a negative answer. Not all Christians can expect to perform these various roles. The same restriction we suggested in the gifts of verses 8–10 seems to apply here: some gifts (in vv. 29, 30) are unique and unrepeatable ("apostle"); others are shared in every age ("helpers"); while some are to be ranked "higher" than others. Those at the end of the list would most naturally be, in Paul's esteem, less important, but evidently they were the very gifts by which the Corinthians set greatest store.

This brings us to a notable crux in verse 31. At face value Paul is thought to be reverting to the gifts at the head of his list. The "greater" (*meizona*) gifts are those that are prominent in 12:8 and

12:28 respectively, while if we look ahead to 14:1 Paul is apparently issuing a call to the reader to "strive for spiritual gifts and especially that you may prophesy." The Greek *meizona* is taken, on this reading, as a genuine comparative, contrasting the more desirable and the less spectacular gifts of the Spirit of gifts-in-grace. But we need to ask if this view is most likely.

This interpretation is by no means the only viable option, and its unsatisfactoriness stems largely from Paul's apparent endorsement of a seeking of spiritual gifts in a community where such an ambition had led to acute problems. Gerhard Iber[11] makes a good point when he remarks that Paul would hardly encourage the Corinthians to strive selfishly after the greatest gifts after he had just admonished them to be content with the gift the Spirit had apportioned to them (12:11) and as God had arranged the body (12:18). The trouble, as we have just observed, is that there was a competitive spirit present and an inordinate desire for members to covet the so-called "greater" gifts. "There was no apparent reason why Paul should strengthen them in this unspiritual striving," comments Bittlinger.[12] "As far as he could see it was their childish immaturity that had made them want the 'greatest' gifts."

Iber's solution is to translate Paul's single Greek word *zēloute* in verse 31 as a statement rather than an imperative: "You are striving after the greatest gifts." As a confirmation of this rendering he appeals to 14:12 where the Corinthians are described as those who are "zealous (*zēlōtai*) for the spirits," that is, spiritual gifts—a designation Paul accepts but then proceeds to challenge by his following remarks. Iber solves the problem in 12:31 by this neat device. He writes:

> The verse then characterizes the attitude of the Corinthian church and expresses succinctly the cause of the apostle's rebuke: that they were striving after the "greatest" gifts.

Two further observations may be made on this eminently reasonable suggestion. David Baker[13] suggests that Paul is here citing from the Corinthians' own statement and so the phrase *"you are seeking the highest gifts"* picks up the Corinthian slogan with the verb "to seek," a word that Paul normally used in a bad sense (1 Cor. 3:3; 13:4; 2 Cor. 12:20; Rom. 13:13; Gal. 4:17; 5:20). His argument includes the suggestion that the key term *pneumatika* (most clearly in 12:1, and implied in 14:12) is also a

Corinthian term that Paul quotes only to modify it by including it (so says M.-A. Chevallier,[14] on whose discussion Baker draws) in the larger scope of *charismata*. Most commentators run these two words together as equivalents, but we have earlier suggested that *pneumatika* relate more to the worship activity of the congregation.

Second, Chevallier draws yet another point of distinction: "So far from linking the charismata with the pneumatika, Paul (in our view) integrates the pneumatika with the charismata" in a special way. He recalls the Corinthian "ambition" for "spiritual experiences," but shifts the emphasis on to these "gifts" as gifts of God, not human opportunities for self-gratification. Thus, Chevallier submits, Paul does something, of which he is elsewhere fond, namely, he takes the point of view of his correspondents but redirects it in a new way. In 12:31 we should therefore render the sense thus:

> "You are seeking, then, the greater(est) gifts, are you?" [*Zēloute* could just as well be an interrogative verb.] "Well," Paul replies, "I will [or I intend to] show you a still better way." [*Kai* in verse 31b may have this sense.][15]

The second part of verse 31 is also a problem, although the sense is tolerably clear. The phrase *kath' hyperbolēn* is usually taken attributively in association with *hodos,* that is, "a more excellent way," but it could be construed as an adverb modifying the verb; so "Beyond all that I have so far said, I show you a way." If we could rely on the variant text-form of P 46 and a Western reading (which has *ei ti* in place of *eti*), then the force of this second translation would be enhanced: if there is anything beyond, I propose to show you the way. That would make even more pointed the contrast between the Corinthians' proposal ("we are seeking the more ecstatic gifts as the 'highest' tokens of divine favor") and Paul's challenge (if their statement is turned by him into a question, as I propose) and counterproposal ("If you are ambitious for *charismata* that you call *pneumatika* [spirit-powers; cf. 14:12], then even if there is anything beyond to which you aspire, I will show you the way to reach that goal").

The "way" is the way of love (*agapē*); the way does not lead to love, for love is not one of the *charismata*. Rather, "love" is the way to that maturity to which the exercise of the *pneumatika* supposedly leads. Here we touch the nerve-center of the debate between Paul and the Corinthian enthusiasts. These believers claimed an excess of *pneumatika* and sought thereby to attain excellence as part of their *gnōsis* and *sophia* religion. Paul concedes the presence of their ambition and their "zeal," but warns them of its misuse when these enthusiasms are misdirected into selfish and unedifying channels. What counts is concern for the entire community (12:7), a contentment with whatever gifts a person has (12:11), and a recognition that not all the gifts are open to all (12:28, 29). This leads him to clinch his argument: any and every charism must be exercised within the encompassing constraint and motivation of *agapē,* which gives worth to all the *charismata.*

Paul will insert chapter 13 as either a preformed hymnic composition or (less likely) an exultant poetic outburst written *currente calamo* to serve as a "bridge" (Chevallier) joining 12:31 and 14:1 where again he will do what he has done before in this epistle. As at 6:12–20 and 7:1–7 he will cite the actual wording of the Corinthians' letter and then proceed to comment on it, with the intention of correcting wrong ideas and impressions.

One remaining item may round off this exposition. In the light of the preceding discussion we are now in a position to ask, What is a *charisma* in Paul's teaching? Doubtless he placed great value on the possession and use of such a "gift" seen as a direct gift from God; and he uses the term both to include the more narrowly defined *pneumatika* (which are more related to worship and were greatly sought after in the Corinthian assembly) and to correct the false notions that had clustered around these "spirit-gifts." For the Corinthians *pneuma* was their chief interest, and Paul has to drive a wedge between aspirations of the human spirit (which may be ill-considered and "fleshly") and the control of the Holy Spirit who is never said to *impart charismata,* only to be the channel through which such gifts proceed from God. Käsemann, in one of his earlier writings, puts the Pauline intention starkly: "Paul seeks to replace the idea of *charismata* by that of *charis,*"[16] that is, a gift directly from God (see 1 Cor. 7:7).

This line of reasoning helps us to elucidate a vexatious question, How far are the charismatic gifts supernatural and how far do they heighten and intensify human endowments? Käsemann is helpful again at this point, which complements his earlier discussion.[17] What counts, he says, is not the mere existence of a *charisma* but "the use to which it is put." The controlling rubric under which a *charisma* is properly exercised is "in the Lord,"[18] a phrase drawn from 1 Corinthians 7:39 (cf. 7:7, where the charism is one of celibacy, which may be replaced by that of marriage). In other words, any condition of life may *become* a person's *charisma* from God "only when I recognize that the Lord has given it to me and that I am to accept this gift as his calling and command to me. Now everything can become for me 'charisma.'" The upshot of this discussion is to lift the Christian's activity out of the sacral-cultic area and relocate it in the mundane or even "profane" world over which Christ rules as Lord of the cosmos. No "gift" is inherently charismatic, but it has the possibility of becoming so if it is claimed and utilized under the domain of Christ. Thus the natural order is "sacralized" by being owned for Christ. The criterion is the lordship of Christ, now seen as a banner covering the most "secular" of activities—eating, drinking, living, dying (Rom. 14:4–23)—as well as a person's marital status (1 Cor. 7). The credal statement of 1 Corinthians 12:3, "Jesus is Lord," is thus the key to Paul's corrective teaching; it warns that since Christ is "cosmocrat" (= world-ruler), no part of life lies outside his dominion, and so every human activity may be recruited to serve the divine purpose, and so become charismatic.

Translation

1–3 If I speak in tongues of mortals and even of angels, and have not love, I have become a resounding gong or a clashing cymbal. If I have the gift of prophecy, and understand all the mysterious secrets and all "knowledge," if I have all kinds of faith so as to move mountains, but have not love, I am nothing. If *I give away* all my possessions *as food portions*[a] [to feed the hungry], if I hand over my body *to be burned*,[b] but have not love, I am not benefited at all.

4–7 Love is patient, love is kind, love is not jealous, does not boast, does not behave itself arrogantly, *does not act shamefully*,[c] does not seek its own advantage, is not irritated, does not *keep a register* of evil,[d] does not rejoice at wickedness but rejoices with the truth. It *puts up with* everything,[e] has faith all the time, is always hopeful, ever enduring.[f]

8–13 Love never fails. If there are prophecies, they will be brought to an end. If tongues, they will cease. If knowledge, it will be brought to an end. Our knowledge is incomplete, our prophesying is incomplete. But when the complete comes, then the incomplete will be brought to an end. When I was an *infant*,[g] I spoke as an infant, I thought as an infant, I reasoned as an infant. Now that I have become a man, I have brought my infantile ways to an end. Now we see (things) in a mirror and obscurely, but then we shall see face to face. Now my knowledge is incomplete, but then I shall know fully just as I am fully known (by God).[h]

So then, *these three* are what lasts:[i] faith, hope, love. But greater than these is the love (of God).[j]

Points to Ponder

a. ψωμίζω, "I give away all my property bit by bit" (ψωμίον): see Gingrich-Danker, *Lexicon,* p. 894, for this sense.

b. ἵνα καυθήσομαι. The variant ἵνα καυχήσωμαι, "that I may boast," is read by P 46 Aleph A B and Nestle[26]. But see G. Zuntz, *The Text of the Epistles* (1953), pp. 35ff. for discussion, maintaining the variant arose in Egypt in the second century.

c. οὐκ ἀσχημονεῖ: a reference to 12:23?

d. A commercial verb: to keep account (λόγος).

e. στέγω has a wide range of meanings. Which is best here?

f. I take πάντα to be adverbial in each case.

g. νήπιος is literally "not able to speak," hence "infant," "babe."

h. Another example of the divine passive.

i. τὰ τρία ταῦτα: "the well-known three," as a catechetical triad. So A. M. Hunter, *Paul and his Predecessors*[2] (1961), 33ff.

j. I have argued for this translation in *The Expository Times* 82 (1971):119, 120.

CHAPTER THREE

IN PRAISE OF LOVE

FORM OF THE PASSAGE

This title has been chosen with an eye to some features that stamp
this particular chapter as almost in a class by itself in the Pauline
literature. Chapter 13 is poetic in its style and carries all the marks
of a lyrical composition: it has a number of *hapax legomena,* words
and phrases found only here; there are unusual examples of sty-
listic-syntactical forms; several word-pictures are mixed together;
the grouping of sentences and words into three's is common; the
main subject, "love," is absolutized; and there is a noticeable
absence of distinctive Christian—and indeed explicit christological—features. To this list (from Wischmeyer)[1] we may add the
way in which the verses may suggestively be set in strophes. There
are three such stanzas (vv. 1–3; 4–7; 8–12 [13]), each with its
own peculiar traits of rhetorical pattern and style. In *stanza I* (vv.
1–3) there is the arrangement of protasis (If . . .) and apodosis
(then. . .). *Stanza II* (vv. 4–7) is full of antithetical and in part
rhymelike clauses. "Love" is the subject throughout, and some
have suggested that this middle part had an independent existence
since it is didactic, not hymnic, in form, and belongs to the Old
Testament paraenetic emphasis as developed in the wisdom school
of intertestamental Judaism (so G. von Rad).[2] It is this central
strophe that most clearly stands in the Jewish wisdom tradition,
which has some notable tributes of praise to "wisdom" (Prov. 8;
Sir. 24; Wis. of Sol. 7). The closest parallel is 3 Ezra 4:34–40
where "truth" is lauded in a remarkable tribute to its strength,
universality, and endurance forever. God is finally praised in this
tribute as "the God of truth."

Stanza III (vv. 8–12[13]) has an opening statement followed by
three anaphoras and three corresponding antistrophic parallelisms
(v. 8); verses 9 and 10 form an antithetic parallelism, with verse 11

an antithesis, and verse 12 a double antithesis. Verse 13 looks to be a statement of the hymn's thesis with a concluding coda.

Throughout the chapter one subject prevails; and this singular concentration on love gives rise to the overall designation of a "Hymn of love," or better, an *aretalogy* (i.e., poetic rhapsody composed in praise of a deity or some attribute regarded as divine) dedicated to *agapē*.

Whatever word we choose to describe this piece, certain observations form a modern consensus: (*i*) it is an independent composition, whether Pauline or not; (*ii*) it is obviously a self-contained unity, and has been inserted between 12:31 and 14:1 either fortuitously (since, Weiss and Conzelmann insist, it is out of place in the flow of Paul's argument here seen in the way that "prophecy" is said to be differently evaluated in 13:2 and 14:1, but the chapter could stand in 1 Cor. 8); or on set purpose (as relevant to the Corinthian situation after Paul's writing ch. 12 [so Barrett]; or "integral to the course of Paul's present argument" [Bruce]; or as directed precisely to a false understanding of *pneumatika* at Corinth [so Wischmeyer]);[3] (*iii*) the ethical teaching in this passage rests on a firm theological base, and the didactic section (vv. 4–7), which has close parallels with the Jewish *Testaments of the Twelve Patriarchs* (*Test. Iss.* 4), is but an example of the Jewish ethical maxim of *imitatio Dei*: that is, God's character is made the norm for moral behavior. The obvious difference from Paul is that for him, whatever may have been his training in the hellenistic Jewish schools, the face of God is inevitably seen in Jesus Christ. So theology merges into christology, not explicitly but by a process of osmosis whereby God's character is set by what he (Paul) had discovered in his encounter and continuing communion with his Lord.

At all events this noble chapter stands as "the greatest, strongest, deepest thing Paul ever wrote" (von Harnack),[4] however we may resolve the literary and form-critical questions.

STANZA 1 (VV. 1–3)

The opening verses stress the *preeminence of love* when set over against certain gifts of the Spirit that were much prized at Corinth. We recall that "love" is not one of other *charismata*; indeed it is not a *charisma* but a fruit of the Spirit (Gal. 5:22f.). Love is, rather, the essential accompaniment of all the gifts. In fact, a gift of the Spirit

gains in value *only* as it is exercised *in love*. Karl Barth's heading[5] for
stanza I is appropriate: love alone counts.

Five gifts are mentioned, each requiring love to be its partner
and controlling force.

(a) *Eloquence and ecstatic speech*: "If I speak in tongues of men and
[even] of angels" suggests a double allusion to rhetorical expertise
such as Apollos commanded (Acts 18:24), and to the glossolalic
gift practiced at Corinth. This is one of the clearest indications
that, even if 1 Corinthians 13 did exist independently, its theme
exactly matches the Corinthian scene, as Conzelmann is bound to
acknowledge. The church at Corinth had an Apollos party (1 Cor.
1:12; 3:4, 22), and it set great store by the charism of "the tongues
of angels," a Jewish phrase to denote a type of prayer-speech
eminently suited to praising God, as the daughters of Job did (*Test.
Job* 48–50). The Corinthians' claim to have facility in this type of
language may betray more than an exuberance and exaltation of
spirit; it may signify a conviction that they had already entered
upon the kingdom age (1 Cor. 4:8) in its fullness, and their
glossolalia was the sign that they believed the eschatological hope
of the future was already made good in their midst. If so, what they
had done was effectively to deny Paul's futurist eschatology and
bring the future into the present in their public worship assemblies, with attendant problems of an overheated excitement (1 Cor.
12:2; cf. 14:40). Paul, as we shall see, gives a measured approval to
glossolalia (14:4, 18, 39), but sets it within the control of his
"eschatological proviso," that is, by stating that the new age is
already here but not yet in its fullness and power. Therefore glossolalia should not be allowed to dominate the scene as if the
eschatological hope had "collapsed" into present experience.

In chapter 13 the emphasis is slightly different: "even if I am
caught up in a trance-like experience, my *eloquence* and my *glossolalia* are to no avail—they are single-toned as a gong or a cymbal
(both musical instruments used in ecstatic cults),[6] not melo-
dious—if love is absent." Already Paul is registering an appeal to
be made in 14:6–12: "tongues" must be regulated to produce not
only sound but sense, that the church as a whole may be edified in
love.

(b) *Intellectual gifts,* of which prophecy is singled out (along with
tongues, but in reverse order in ch. 14), stand next in the list. The
link with "mysteries" and "knowledge" shows that Paul is talking

descriptively about "wisdom" in the sense of 12:8. These terms refer to Spirit-inspired utterances made by individuals in the community, giving insight into the mind and plan of God for the community (see 1 Cor. 2:7 for Paul's own possession of this ability). But the link with glossolalia is clear from 14:2: "he speaks mysteries in the Spirit." One would have thought that this ministry was in no way objectionable. Yet Paul evidently sensed the danger, when the gifted prophet exercises his ministry to his own advantage (14:2, 4: "he edifies himself") and not "in love," that is, for the well-being of the congregation (exactly as in 1 Cor. 8:1). Then the prophet's word is misdirected and goes beyond the "rule of faith" (Rom. 12:6), where "faith" may well be the form of Christian teaching contained in the baptismal confession of unity in love (Eph. 4:4, 5, 13, 16). Prophecy without love corresponds to prophecy without faith (Rom. 12:6), says Wischmeyer. So it is not *gnōsis* but *agapē* that is for Paul the right Christian life-style.

(c) *Faith*. The Pauline stress on "faith" as containing the quintessence of human response to God's grace is well known (Gal. 5:6; 1 Thess. 1:3; 5:8). A helpful distinction, however, has been drawn between "saving" faith (*Kerygmaglaube*) by which people believe the gospel, and "miracle-working" faith (*Wunderglaube*)[7] such as the exercise of trust that leads God's power to flow in healing (1 Cor. 12:9). It seems clear that Paul has the latter sense in view in 13:2. Only here does he write of "all faith" (*pasa pistis*) as if to draw attention to that faith which accomplishes great results. He is perhaps relying on the gospel tradition (Mark 11:22ff.) and especially on Jesus' evoking this response (Matt. 17:20; 21:21). But in any case, the comparison of the special gift of faith to a miraculous force that "removes mountains" makes use of a Jewish proverbial phrase. After an elaborate build-up in the protasis—"if I have gifts of knowledge and the possession of wonder-working faith that can achieve the impossible [which is what the removing of mountains means], yet do not have love," then—"nothing I am" (*ouden eimi*), a powerful anticlimax and memorable apodosis.

(d) *Philanthropy*. The scope of Paul's list changes now to one of personal achievements rather than personal possessions ("I have"). The emphasis falls on what a person does with his possessions. In the first case, he is willing to turn all his property into fragments of food (*psōmos/psōmion*) with a view to distributing such morsels (like the "sop" at the Last Supper meal in John 13:26f., 30) to the poor.

Such charitable concern is altogether praiseworthy (see Acts 4:36, 37; Gal. 2:10), but the motive is the all-important consideration, as we may infer from the warning story of Acts 5:1–11; on the positive side we may compare 1 John 3:17 and 18.

The reference to a Christian's body in the next line could suggest that a person may be willing to surrender his costliest possession, namely, his life. We know of some early Christians who sold themselves into slavery in order to relieve the needy with the money the slavemasters paid for them (1 Clem. 55:2). But Paul's retort is appropriate: What advantage is gained if the motive is wrong? The forfeiture of one's possessions recalls both the gospel scenes of the disciples who "gave up" their livelihood to follow in Jesus' mission and also—as K. Beyschlag and G. Theissen[8] have stressed—the apostolic example in 1 Corinthians 9:4 and 12 of self-renunciation of rights. The disciples professed to have obeyed the call: "We have left everything to follow you!" (Mark 10:28), and Paul's self-abnegation was made in the service of the gospel. His criterion remains that of altruistic "love," but, as Wischmeyer says, this is not only to be understood ethically; it has, as we shall see, a christological dimension in terms of Paul's apostolate set under the authority of the crucified Christ.

(e) *Sacrifice* is the ultimate extent of an individual's self-giving: the subject portrays "man—and, indeed, the *homo religiosus Christianus*—in his highest possibilities,"[9] who is yet ready to lay down his life in martyrdom. He is willing to surrender his body to the flames (reading *kauthēsomai,* which is challenged by the set of early and well-attested readings that give "that I may glory" [*kauchēsōmai*]). The rule of intrinsic probability operates here, as does Bengel's axiom of *lectio difficilior potior* (the more difficult reading is to be preferred). It is more understandable for a scribe to have changed the forceful "that I may be burned." The Old Testament illustration is Daniel 3:28 (cf. 3:95 in the appended Song of the Three, where the LXX and Theodotion have allusions to "fire," as Riesenfeld notes),[10] comparable with the Maccabean martyrs (2 Macc. 7:37; 4 Macc. 18:3) who chose death by burning in Antiochus' persecution rather than an easy compromise of their faith. But the choice of a martyr's death in this way is not only Judeo-Christian: such a brave witness is a set theme in Greco-Roman philosophy, and there was the Indian mystic in Athens who perished in the flames, just as in our generation Buddhist monks dramatized their protest in the petrol fires of Saigon, Vietnam.

Paul's climactic conclusion picks up the earlier mention in verse 2: to achieve the seemingly impossible ("remove mountains") is matched, as Bornkamm remarks,[11] by an attempt to display superhuman courage in martyrdom. In both cases the impressive symmetry ends with a note of futility—"I am nothing"; "I am nothing advantaged"—if love is not the controlling force. What the Corinthians must learn is that faith, whether altruistic or sacrificial, serves no final end unless it is "made operative by love" (Gal. 5:6). This is Paul's counterthrust to Corinthian enthusiasm as he draws examples from the Jewish hortatory tradition. The conclusion at the end of stanza I stands in all its monumental simplicity and direct appeal: "The vanity of all values without love" (Bornkamm). Paul's last word is "profit" (*ōphelein*), which runs parallel with *oikodomē,* upbuilding, a word used often in chapter 14, but not of the pneumatic Christian; rather, it is the community that is central. The contrast, then, is not one of "external action" versus "inner disposition," as A. Fridrichsen supposes;[12] it is more a contrast between what serves to exalt the private individual and his or her own religious experience and that person's concern for the well-being of the entire community.

STANZA II (VV. 4–7)

Karl Barth's heading is once more to the point: it is love alone that triumphs. Paul uses some fifteen verbs to express in four verses the "nature and reign of love" (Bornkamm). The pattern, in fact, is contained in the multiplicity of the verbs, reminding us that love is known by what it does, not what it is *in abstracto.* This observation is a timely statement since it recalls that "love" as a semantic term can never be taken for granted. Its meaning is chameleonlike, changing its color and texture according to its use and context. So we need to have it defined, and can test it against the character of Jesus himself, whose mirror image we see in these verses. Paul gives us three "aspects" of the picture, turning the word *agapē* in several directions so that its scintillating colors may shine in their brilliance. But throughout, the focus is on love that is known by its activity. We do not evaluate it statically as we do a museum piece or an object on a pedestal. Paul manages to "catch" the picture of love in a freeze-frame as its activity unfolds before his eyes.

In effect, Paul says three things about love-in-operation. First, on the positive side, he begins the catalog of what love *does* by listing two verbs: to be patient (*makrothymei*) and to be kind (*chrēsteuetai*). These attributes are partners elsewhere for Paul where the combined forces of these virtues are equally the fruit of the Spirit (Gal. 5:22), a sign of God's election (Col. 3:12), and a method of evangelism (2 Cor. 6:6). The two qualities are Christlike in the literal sense (see Matt. 11:28–30; 2 Cor. 10:1, where the terms are different, however); and they are also Godlike. "Patience"—literally, "far from wrath"—is what God's nature displays in his dealings with people (Rom. 2:4; 1 Pet. 3:20; 2 Pet. 3:9, 15), especially in their rebellion: so Exodus 34:6f. which couples "patient" with "full of mercy" (*polyeleos*, LXX). God's being "slow to anger" is characteristic in the Old Testament (Num. 14:18; Pss. 25:6–10; 84:11ff.; 85:5, 15; 103:4–8; Jonah 4:2) and especially in the Wisdom literature (Wis. Sol. 15:1ff. and the *Testaments of the Twelve Patriarchs, Gad* 4:7; *Jos.* 2:7). In the *Testament of Job* (21:3; 26:5; 27:7) tested "patience" is a function of love and is highly regarded. This is a basic presupposition of the Pauline list of terms, as Wischmeyer says. [13]

It is the same with "kindness," which epitomizes God's dealing with humankind (Rom. 2:4; 11:22; cf. Eph. 2:7; Tit. 3:4). The "generous" spirit is well commended in Judaism (Aboth 6:6) and is seen in forgiveness, as God is gracious to the undeserving (a thought basic to Jesus' teaching; Luke 6:35). "As you show kindness, so will you receive kindness" (1 Clem. 13:2) is cited as an unwritten "word of the Lord" in the spirit of the Golden Rule. *Chrēstos* as a Christian virtue has a verbal echo with *Christos,* "Christ"—a confusion that is visible in some uncials of 1 Peter 2:3 (citing Ps. 34:9) and in a natural mistake of *Chrestus* for *Christus* made by Suetonius (*Life of Claudius* 25:4: "Because the Jews of Rome were indulging in constant riots at the instigation of Chrestus, Claudius expelled them"). Justin (*First Apology* 4) makes capital of this assonance: "As far as the name charged against us goes, we are very gracious people. . . . For we are accused of being Christians; and it is not right to hate graciousness [*chrēston*]"; cf. Tertullian (*Apol.* 3:5).

These two qualities therefore complement each other. Love inspires people to be patient, with a long temper and a slowness to anger, and a restraint when other people's behavior may cause irritation, William Barclay[14] comments; it has less to do with a passivity that gives in to adverse circumstances. Kindness is a natural partner, offering a positive counterbalance, that is, a determination to do people good and seek their positive welfare. Both ideas are rooted in the Old Testament characterization of Yahweh, God of the covenant.

Second, Paul turns his attention to what *love avoids doing*. He offers a series of impressive negatives in verses 5–7 in what may be called an exposition of the abstinence motif, steering Christians away from what is unfitting or may deny their life in Christ, the Lord of love. There is a catalog of eight verbs, each preceded by a negative:

> v. .4. Love is not jealous;
>   Love is not boastful or puffed up in arrogance;
> v. 5. Love is not rude; it is not self-seeking;
>   Love is not irritable; it keeps no record of wrongs;
> v. 6. Love does not rejoice at wrong,
>   but rejoices in the right.

"Jealous" (*zēloi*) recalls that the term may be used in either a positive (Hebrew sense of "zeal" for God) or a negative way. The latter is more frequent in Paul's writing, as we can see from 2 Corinthians 12:20, Galatians 5:20, as well as 1 Corinthians 3:3. Sometimes the meaning is unclear (e.g., 1 Cor. 12:31; 14:1, 12, 39). Wischmeyer correctly observes the ambivalence and remarks that, in view of the dual meanings (a wrongful jealously of one's neighbor, and pneumatic "zeal") that are closely associated by Paul, we must hear his criticism of any "zeal" that fails to build up the community.

The next verb, which is extremely rare, describes the braggart. H. Braun[15] connects this haughty attitude with what was going on in Corinth, especially the arrogance of the members who boasted, "I have no need of you" (1 Cor. 12:21); it may also deal with the Corinthian sophistry in speech (1 Cor. 1:17; 2:1ff.).

"Not puffed up" suggests the presence of a "wind-bag" inflated with his own importance, and we may be tempted to dismiss it as an eccentricity. But more than that is at stake, as we see from the

use of the verb in those chapters dealing with moral issues at
Corinth (4:6 against party rivalry; 4:18, 19 against the spirit of
pride in *gnōsis*). "Being inflated," we may conclude, was the cardinal symptom of the serious malaise afflicting the Corinthian
church, and it stems from their wrong-headed notions about their
present position as "risen and reigning with Christ" (4:8). They
thought of themselves as already enjoying the fullness of the new
age here and now, with its invitation to libertinism and resulting
in a proud bypassing of the kerygma of the cross whose token was
Christ's humiliation (*tapeinophrosynē*), and the apostle's corresponding weakness-in-him (2 Cor. 12:20, 21; 13:4).

Moral blemishes in the Corinthian church showed themselves in
"rudeness" (lit., love "does not act in an unseemly way," either by
thoughtlessness, taking advantage of another person [7:36], plain
violation of good taste at the agape meal [11:20–22], or anarchical
behavior in services of worship [14:31–40]). Love is never guilty of
improper conduct, since that would deny the *koinōnia* intended to
bind Christians together in a bodily harmony where the "weaker"
and "less presentable" (*aschēmona*: a play on the verb here, *aschēmonei*) parts do not feel embarrassed by the haughty or careless
actions of the prominent members. In spite of the suggestion that
here we see Paul calling on a set "vice list" (Rom. 1:27ff.), clearly
he does have the Corinthian situation well in his sights.

"Seeking one's own" means again "insisting on one's own way,"
like the erring Philippians who are rebuked in Philippians 2:1–4
(cf. Phil. 2:21) as well as the Corinthian readers already addressed
in 1 Corinthians 10:24 and 33. Such ambition has to be directed by
love to serve the highest interests of one's neighbor, even if those
interests are in conflict with a person's own goals and preferences.
The christological motive may well be seen in the background
here, since Paul elsewhere sets out the "choice" of Christ in his
incarnation and condescension as a paradigm of Christian behavior. Not that we can do as he did. Rather, the call is that we
conform our life-style to the pattern of self-abnegation he has set
(Rom. 15:2f.; Phil. 2:6–8; 2 Cor. 8:9).

Paroxynein ("to incite") can be taken in two quite opposite ways,
as either a good emulation prompted by love (Heb. 10:24) or a bad
altercation (Acts 15:39). In the context of 1 Corinthians 13 the
connection with "to be jealous" is clear, and Paul's use is pejorative. So he writes: love "is not provoked to anger" by resent-

ment (as in the case of Korah in Num. 16:30 LXX, *paroxynein*, an attitude that is joined in Num. 17:6 with grumbling, *goggyzein*, a verb associated with the Corinthians' disaffection according to 1 Cor. 10:10).

So far the six verbs unite to form a coherent profile of the troubles at Corinth, and Paul submits a theological critique in the name of *agapē*. At the heart of the nest of pastoral problems was a theological error—the claim to *gnōsis*—and Paul's corrective is expressed in equally singular terms: it is the pattern and driving force of love that can keep these vices far from the Christian and replace them by active goodwill.

Two remaining verbs in verse 6 clinch the matter in a more general way. For one thing, Paul has recourse to the Old Testament, citing Zechariah 8:17 and drawing on a commercial terminology. Love does not "keep a register" of wrongs, storing up a memory bank of evils allegedly committed with a view to paying back the offender in his own coin. The Pauline verb *logizesthai* plays a prominent role in the apostle's teaching on justification by faith, since God does not "reckon" trespasses to sinners but freely pardons in grace and sets men and women in a right relationship with himself (Rom. 4). Thus love is brought within the orbit of Paul's justification teaching, and the summons is implicit: act as God does.

"Not delighting in *evil* but rejoicing in the *truth*" sets two moral values in antithesis (as in Rom. 1:18; 2:8; 2 Thess. 2:12). The negative stance love adopts may suggest a refusal to be drawn in to evil complicity or else a holding aloof from a censorious attitude, not being glad when others go wrong (so Moffatt's translation). Love is "gladdened by goodness" wherever and whenever it appears. Paul's generous spirit shines out here; and for a practical illustration we may point to Philippians 1:15–18 where Paul will rejoice even if there are those who bear him no goodwill or love, yet are nevertheless proclaiming Christ. His own reputation is of less account than the progress of God's work, no matter who is engaged in it (see 2 Cor. 6:6–8).

Third, verse 7 summarizes, telling us what *love does continually*. In a series of short sentences, formulated with artistic intention to produce the rhythm of identical endings (*epiphora*), and each commencing with a fourfold repetition (*panta*), the verse has a memorable cadence. Love has qualities of which we have heard in the previous part of the strophe; now Paul will stress that these are no ephemeral or changeable attitudes and actions. They last on . . . or they "never fail" or fall down through weakness or disinclination or frustration as verse 8a will conclude. Instead, love has an enduring quality, if we are correct in taking *panta* to mean not "all things" but in an adverbial sense of "always." So we could render: "there is nothing love cannot face; there is no limit to its faith, its hope, and its endurance" (NEB).

The verb *stegei* has given rise to diverse translations: always protects (NIV); always slow to expose (Moffatt); bears all things (RSV); supports all things (Barrett); draws a veil of silence over all, covers everything (Conzelmann); "bears" = "holds up all things" (Vulgate *omnia suffert*) or even "puts up with everything." The idea of endurance is presumably what the last verb (*hypomenei*) implies, so Paul can hardly be tautologous, yet *stegein* can mean just that (1 Cor. 9:12). F. F. Bruce and Weiss appeal to 1 Peter 4:8 for the nuance, "love *covers* all things unworthy, instead of exposing them or blazing them abroad"; then the action is one of discretion, not cowardly unconcern. C. K. Barrett offers "support" with a reference to the Jewish rabbinic teaching that Torah, Temple, and alms-giving hold the world in place (Aboth 1:2), a suggestive parallel since Paul would then be substituting love for the essence of Judaism.

On the other side, Wischmeyer[16] makes a good case for treating *stegei* in light of the same verb's usage in 1 Corinthians 9:12. She argues that the constant reference to "all" (eight times in 1 Cor. 13:1–7) is not accidental but polemical. Paul is directing his shafts against the realized eschatologists at Corinth whose watchword is heard in 1 Corinthians 4:8: they professed that they had begun to reign already; hence, "all things are permitted" is their passport to ethical freedom (1 Cor. 6:12). This faulty eschatology coupled with libertine ethics is judged by Paul in the light of his teaching on "not yet"; thus the verbs "hoping," believing," and "enduring" in verse 7. Moreover, the slogan "all things are lawful" (*panta exestin*) is countered by Paul's self-imposed restriction: "I put up with all things" and curtail my freedom as befits my existence in the interim between the now and the then of final redemption.

The other verbs in verse 7 are less problematical. Love "trusts" (is ready to believe the best, is not unduly suspicious); "hopes" even when hope seems foolhardy and beyond all credibility, as

Abraham typified (Rom. 4:18); "endures" to the end with a quality of rugged perseverance (Rom. 12:12) when tempted to quit in
despair. Faith/hope/endurance all merge into a unified picture
that is completed by Paul's final verb: "love never disappears." If
Wischmeyer's analysis given above is plausible, then the apostolic
debate with the Corinthian enthusiasts continues. Paul—speaking
in the name of love—"suffers" while they profess to have reached
the goal of perfection (1 Cor. 4:8; a central statement in Schrage's
reconstruction of the Corinthians' manifesto).[17] Love maintains
"trust" as a direct opposite to "walking by sight" in a realized
kingdom (2 Cor. 5:7). Love "hopes" in contradiction to the Corinthians for whom all is already in their grasp (1 Cor. 4:7). Love's
restraining "patience" stands in tension with the claim to have all
"authority" (*exousia*) with no limits (1 Cor. 6:12; 10:23). The
Corinthians "have" the *charismata* already in firm possession
(1 Cor. 13:1–3); Paul holds the "gifts of the Spirit" existentially
as is appropriate to the time of waiting for the end.

The attraction of this understanding of stanza II is that it turns
Paul's citation of the hymn into a polemical rebuke (in keeping
with his use of other hymns such as Phil. 2:6–11; Col. 1:15–20),
and does not require us to give only a generalized ethical setting to
his writing. The kerygmatic function of "love" is made the apostolic criterion; and that role makes it easier to see how Paul's
christology is determinative throughout, not some vague assort-
ment of attributes, even if they are associated with love. "Love" as
he perceived it was the test by which he evaluated the Corinthians'
misunderstandings of the *charismata,* or better, the *pneumatika* on
which their hearts were set. Even worse, their misplaced eschatology contributed to a defective understanding of Christ the
Lord whose role as salvation-bringer embodied all the "higher
gifts" appropriate to the period "between the times" of initial
redemption and the arrival of the final phase (called "the perfect"
in v. 10). To Paul's eschatological revision, so badly needed at
Corinth, we turn in stanza III.

STANZA III (VV. 8–12)

The accent here falls on the permanence of love, as Barth again
rightly notes: it is *agapē* alone that endures. Love is set within a
framework of time as Paul contrasts "the already" and "the then."

The distinction is clearly made in verse 12: "*now* my knowledge is incomplete, but *then* I shall know fully just as I am fully known [by God]." More contrasts are seen in the "child"—"adult" image of verse 11, and in the "mirror" that shows only baffling reflections and the "vision" that is face to face in verse 12. Obviously Paul wants to drive home a central point; and it is evident he is in a continuing polemical mood.

"There is, apart from xv., no chapter in the whole Epistle wherein Paul has expressed in such radical terms, and with such incisive severity, what he had to urge in a critical spirit against the Corinthian Christians," writes Barth.[18] But, we may inquire, what is the ground of his criticism? Paul opens with the salvo of his declared principle: love never "fails" (v. 8)—a verb that may mean no more than fail to maintain its strength and appeal, and so "never ends" (RSV, Bruce). That would be true, and Shakespeare's *Sonnet* 116 gives the moralizing interpretation in some well-known lines:

> . . . love is not love
> Which alters when it alteration finds,
> Or bends with the remover to remove.
> O no, it is an ever-fixed mark
> That looks on tempests and is never shaken;
> . . . .
> Love alters not with his brief hours and weeks,
> But bears it out even to the edge of doom.

A true sentiment, to be sure; but is it Paul's point? Rather we should take our cue from the adverb in verse 13: *nyni de*, "*And now* remain faith, hope, love; these are the three." Paul seems to be summing up in a logical manner, though each phrase is slanted in a polemical direction and, as Wischmeyer shows, has the Corinthian situation in view. What was being debated at Corinth and Paul's response thereto is the aim of his concluding summary.

We must now retrace Paul's argument in stanza III and see how he tackles the Corinthian misunderstanding that is centered in the prominence given to *gnōsis*. The three gifts prized by the Corinthian enthusiasts culminate in their possession of "knowledge" (v. 8). Paul counters this claim in several ways: (*i*) our present "knowledge" is partial; (*ii*) like "prophecy" and "tongues" this gift is destined to pass away—at the parousia of Christ, "when the perfect comes"; (*iii*) claiming to have power of "knowledge" is a mark of immaturity; it means acting like a "child" who has not yet attained adulthood, but who imagines that he "knows it all" even though he is a minor (a contrast renewed in 14:20); and (*iv*) most damaging of all, as Paul has already insisted (1 Cor. 8:1), this kind of "knowledge" inflates the individual with inordinate pride. True "knowledge" is that referred to in verse 12. It is God's relationship to his people that calls out their response. He is said to "know" them, that is, to accept them as his own, a term applicable to both now and eternity. They rejoice in the privilege of being "known" by God.

On every count, it seems that the very gifts the Corinthians valued most highly were, in Paul's esteem, to be ranked at a low level. On the contrary, "love" shines as the excellent quality that reaches out to the eschatological future and has the hallmark that sets it above the possession and exercise of the *charismata* even if those "gifts" fulfill a necessary function now. The "gifts," provided they are controlled by love, belong to the present age—and Paul shortly will be concerned to set them in order of priority; only love can be called "the bond of perfection" (Col. 3:14), and it will never disappear.

Then, as all the gifts need love to be properly exercised, it follows that love is greater. It may be said that for Paul the "fruit of the Spirit" (Gal. 5:22, 23) are in a class greater than the "gifts of the Spirit"; and so the Corinthians need to cultivate such fellowship inspired by the Spirit that the "gifts" on which they had set their hearts are not allowed to take too prominent a place or be valued for their own sakes. Only love is self-evidently a Christian quality; all the *charismata* gain validity and value by the use to which they are put, as E. Käsemann remarked (see earlier). They have no independent status; love alone has since it shares the divine perfection (v. 10).

So we reach the puzzling verse 13. Two exegetical observations will orient us to the central problem, which may be stated thus: Is love not only superior to the *charismata* but greater than "faith" and "hope," and if so, how so? A quick answer to that query may be given. Yes, love is the greatest of all attributes since faith and hope will be fulfilled in eternity while love is eternal, and while faith and hope are essential ingredients of the Christian's existence only God may be said to be "love" (1 John 4:8)—a theological appeal Wischmeyer rightly rejects,[19] not because it is wrong, but because it fails to respect the eschatological structure of Paul's thinking here. Is there a better way to set "love" over against the other terms?

First, the phrase "faith, hope, love" looks to be a preformed triad of Christian "virtues" attested in Paul, who in turn derived it from his predecessors, and in other Christian literature (1 Thess. 1:3; 5:8; Col. 1:3f.; Rom. 5:3ff.; cf. Gal. 5:5, 6; Eph. 4:2–5 in the Pauline corpus; and in the NT elsewhere Heb. 6:10–12; 10:22–24; 1 Pet. 1:3–8, 21f.; outside the NT Barn. 1:4; 11:8; Polycarp, *Phil.* 3:2f.). The expression reads here in a way that suggests that Paul is appealing to a well-known formula. "Faith, hope, love"—these, you know, are "the three" traditional qualities that mark out the life of the Christian. The singular verb, "remains" (*menei*), confirms the citation of a formula.

Second, what of the adjective *meizōn?* Normally this comparative form is rendered as a superlative, according to the principle that in hellenistic Greek, *meizōn* took on this meaning in place of *megistos,* the true superlative. So all translations render: love is the great*est* of the trio. *Toutōn,* "of these," is partitive genitive. But could it be that we should retain the comparative sense, thus reading *toutōn* as genitive of comparison? Then, we translate: The triad remains, but greater than these [human qualities] is the love [of God]. The chapter, I suggest,[20] ends on a note of unexpected climax, as Paul appeals to the divine love seen in Jesus Christ who has certainly been at the center of Paul's "lyric of love" throughout.

If this suggestion holds—or indeed if we champion the traditional view that it is the human experience of and response to love that really matters in this chapter—the fact remains that Christ himself is at the heart of the apostle's discussion.[21] "We do not know what love is till we see it in Jesus," James Denney reminds us; furthermore, "when we see it there we see Him identifying Himself with God's interest in us."[22]

Love (*agapē*) may now be defined, though the term is elusive. It denotes a caring attitude and an outgoing action to those in need (as in Luke 10:25–37, the kind Samaritan story); it is, says Lewis Smedes, help to one's neighbor with no expectation of reward.[23] But Denney[24] gets really to the heart of the issue. He quotes a source as saying that love "is the identification of ourselves with God's interest in others." And that identification can only be seen in a christological-soteriological light. Love is what God in Christ has shown and done for "others" in their helpless plight and hapless estate as sinners. In love we take God's side, share his outlook, and implement his designs; and we treat our neighbors as we know God has treated us (see Rom. 15:1–7).

Where the Corinthians had signally failed was (*i*) in despising "love" in their preference for "knowledge" (and its attendant *charismata* of "prophecy" and "tongues"), which led to pride, self-importance, and a demeaning of other members of the body; (*ii*) in claiming, on the ground of a faulty eschatology, that their present "knowledge," with their "tongues," was a token that the kingdom-age had already arrived in its completeness and they were "reigning" (1 Cor. 4:8) now. They therefore believed the selected *charismata* were permanent and eternal; (*iii*) in failing to set the lordship of the crucified Jesus at the center, they had no criterion to test their effusive experiences. Perhaps they retorted to Paul that they *did* know the current formula: "faith, hope, love." What they missed was to set "love" at its head since Christ's love is the only constraining force (2 Cor. 5:14) that can enable a person to break out of the imprisoning circle of egocentricity and selfish pride and have a "genuine concern" (1 Cor. 12:25) for one's neighbor.

So love is paramount on every score; and not least because it is of the very essence of Christian existence both now and forever. This chapter stands out, as Wischmeyer says,[25] as the center of Paul's theology; and it is an exquisite blend of christology, soteriology, and ethics.

Translation

1–9 Make [*this kind of*]ᵃ love your goal; yet "*you are striving for spiritual gifts,*"ᵇ but [I say] rather *that you should all prophesy.*ᶜ For the one who speaks in a tongue speaks not to men but to God, for no one understands [him]. He speaks mystic secrets by inspiration. On the other hand, the one who prophesies speaks to people with a view to their building up, encouragement, and comfort. The one who speaks in a tongue builds up himself; the one who prophesies builds up the community. I want you all to speak in tongues, but much rather that you should prophesy.

He who prophesies is greater than he who speaks in tongues, unless indeed he interprets, that the church may receive something to build it up. *So then,*ᵈ brothers, if I come to you speaking in tongues, how shall I benefit you, unless I speak to you by words of revelation or of knowledge or of prophecy or of teaching?

*In the same way,*ᵉ if lifeless objects which give a sound—a flute or a harp—do not give a distinction in the tones, how will the tune played on the flute or the harp be recognized? And if the trumpet gives an indistinct sound, who will prepare for battle? In the same way, unless you utter clear speech with your tongue, how will what you are saying be recognized? You will be speaking into the air!

10–19 There are, *I suppose,*ᶠ innumerable kinds of sound in the world, and *none of them is meaningless.*ᵍ So unless I know the meaning of the sound, I shall be a *barbarian*ʰ to the speaker, and the speaker will be as a barbarian to me.

So you too, since you are eager-in-striving-forⁱ spiritual [gifts], seek to excel for the building up of the church. Therefore let the one who speaks in a tongue pray that he may interpret.

If I pray in a tongue, my spirit prays, but my mind is inactive. What is to be done then [about this situation]?ʲ I will pray with the/my spirit, but I will pray with my mind *as well.*ᵏ I will sing praise with the/my spirit, but I will praise with my mind as well.

If you, then, give thanks in the spirit, how will the person who takes the place of the *inquirer*ˡ say the Amen to your thanksgiving, since he does not know what you are saying? You give thanks splendidly, but the other person is not built up. I thank [my] Godᵐ that I speak in tongues more than you all. But in the assembled community I prefer to speak five words using my mind, that I may instruct others *as well,*ⁿ rather than thousands of words in a tongue.

20–25 Brothers, do not be children in your thinking. In [the matter of] evil be *infants,*º but in your thinking be mature. It is written in the law:

> I shall speak to this people by men of other tongues and by the lips of others
> But even so they will not heed me, says the Lord.

So "tongues" *are*ᴾ for a sign not to believers but to unbelievers, but prophecy is not for unbelievers but for believers.

If therefore the entire congregation assembles together and all speak with tongues, and inquirers and unbelievers come in, will they not say that you are "possessed"? But if everyone prophesies, and an unbeliever or an inquirer comes in, he is convicted by all, he is tested by all, and so the hidden things of his heart are brought to light. Thus, falling on his face he will *worship*q God, declaring "God is truly in your midst."

Points to Ponder

a. The definite article τὴν ἀγάπην will refer back to 13:13, in my view.

b. Note ζηλοῦτε, "you are striving," here and the use in 14:12 of ζηλωταί. Hence I suggest it is here a citation of the Corinthians' position, which Paul corrects.

c. Paul's corrective, with ἵνα the imperatival use. See H. G. Meecham, *Journal of Theological Studies* 43 (1942): 179f.

d. νυνὶ δὲ, a logical connection.

e. Reading ὁμῶς rather than ὅμως, "nevertheless"; cf. Gal. 3:15.

f. Translating εἰ τύχοι parsed as a "potential optative" mood; cf. 15:37.

g. Or "no nation [ἔθνος] of them [the world] is speechless." So Lietzmann.

h. βάρβαρος, one whose speech sounded like "bar-bar" to the Greek ear.

i. Refer to 14:1 for ζηλωταί.

j. Translating τί οὖν ἐστιν; lit. "What then is it?"

k. One of the few instances in the NT where the καί is significant.

l. ἰδιώτης, a difficult word: lit. "a nonexpert" but here an inquirer (based on synagogue practice) or a nonecstatic (Conzelmann).

m. A rare case of Paul's "[my] God" suggesting his description of private religious experience.

n. See k above.

o. νήπιος: lit. "not able to speak," suggesting an improper use of tongues leading to bad consequences.

p. εἰσιν: an exegetical use of the verb "to be" = represent, stand for, referring to OT scriptural proof (cf. 2 Cor. 3:17, 18). If so, verse 22 refers to OT persons. "Believers" = Israel, "unbelievers" = Assyrians.

q. Worship in the OT implies prostration (Heb. hištaḥᵃwāh). See "Obeisance," in *The International Standard Bible Encyclopedia*, vol. 3 (forthcoming).

CHAPTER FOUR

PROPHESYING, PRAISING, PRAYING

INTRODUCTION

First Corinthians 14:1–25 is a difficult passage, but at least the main headings are clear. Paul is talking about three parts of early Christian worship as these items contribute to the total picture of the things that went on when the primitive believers gathered for corporate worship. Here is our first vital clue to the meaning of the passage. Paul is not addressing the inner meaning of what the worship of God should be to the individual, except only incidentally (14:2, 4, 28). Rather, the scope of his vision—and so the intent of his admonition—is related to the whole congregation at public assembly.

The closest parallels we have to Paul's descriptions of Corinthian worship are drawn from Jewish worship in the synagogue. As far as we can piece together the format of synagogue worship, three elements stand out: the praise of God, and the reading and exposition of Scripture, both enclosed within a framework of united prayer. Though there is some current discussion on how far our knowledge of Jewish worship in the first century A.D. extends, the primary emphasis does seem clearly to fall on *praise,* whether of the "berakah" (lit. "blessing" God) type or the "hodayah," which means more properly thanksgiving to God for his mercies. There is also an "anamnesis" type of prayer by which the goodness of Israel's God is "remembered" and his saving favors to the nation and individuals relived. Scripture, read and applied, was given a central place side by side with praise, although in public worship the reading of Scripture was accorded precedence over the rabbis' homily. Paul F. Bradshaw sums up:

> These considerations [of the various yet essential ways the Hebrew Scriptures were read on the basis of a *lectio continua* on set days in the

calendar] . . . point to the conclusion that the ministry of the word was not seen as an integral element in the act of worship but rather as an occasional appendix to it, made simply for the sake of convenience, because the congregation happened to be gathered together already.[1]

On the basis of his study, Bradshaw writes of three elements in the daily devotion of every pious Jew, reflected in synagogue worship: the orderly and continuous study of the Scriptures, the *shema* (or confession of faith), and the *tefillah* (or daily prayers). If we confine our interest to 1 Corinthians 14, we can see some apparent links, but we must also recognize major differences. In particular, Paul's writing is confronting a scene of unbridled enthusiasm and absence of "order." To anticipate our conclusion, it seems that Paul wants to inject some semblance of "control" and "order" (14:32, 33, 40) into this situation. His discussion reflects his cultural bias derived from the synagogue as well as his concern to keep worship within set limits that promote "reverence" (14:25). His rubrics or signpost words are therefore a necessary preamble to our understanding of his mind.

PAUL'S CONTROLS

(a) We remind ourselves—because this is the theme Paul keeps returning to in 14:1–40—that we are looking at *the church gathered for and practicing worship in the public assembly*. Consider the following:

> "In the church" (*en ekklēsia*) (v. 19)
> "In the church" (*en ekklēsia*) (v. 28)
> "When/if the whole church comes together" (*synelthē*) (v. 23)
> "When you come together" (*synerchēsthe*) (v. 26)
> "It is disgraceful for a woman to speak in the church" (*en ekklēsia*)
>   (v. 35)

And with an alternative translation:

> "God is not a God of disorder but of peace, as in all the congregations (*en pasais tais ekklēsiais*) of the saints" (v. 33)

(b) The central motif, given this context of the entire assembly met together, is not surprisingly *one of "upbuilding"* (*oikodomē*), which Paul goes out of his way to insist on, both negatively (14:17: "the other person is not edified") and, more emphatically, positively:

The prophet speaks [unlike the tongue-speaker who builds up himself, v. 4a] . . . to the congregation for its . . . strengthening [lit. *oikodomē*, upbuilding, v. 3] and builds up the community [v. 4b]. [The latter course is clearly preferred.]

Paul qualifies his demotion of the glossolalic who speaks "in private"; but if there is a corresponding interpretation given to what is now obviously a tongue offered "in public," then the desired effect of worship is secured: "so that the church may be edified" (v. 5). "Excellent gifts," Paul comments, carry this hallmark: they build up the church (v. 12). Whatever contributions are brought to the service, their value stands under this banner: "all of these must be done for the strengthening (*oikodomē*) of the church" (v. 26).

Paul's teaching on *oikodomē* can hardly be exaggerated, and several students have noted the stress on the well-being and growth of the entire fellowship, as opposed to the Corinthians' desire to turn the church into a Gnostic conventicle of private individuals, each concerned with his or her own inalienable experiences and heedless of the corporate dimension (what we surnamed "body life" in ch. 2) as *a Pauline distinctive*. Failure to observe the designation "one body, one Spirit" (1 Cor. 12:12, 13) had led to much mischief at Corinth; and this fault was never more glaringly and tragically obvious than at public worship and at the Lord's Supper table (1 Cor. 11:17–34).

(c) Yet one more apostolic injunction was called for at Corinth, in the light of the chaotic conditions that prevailed at the worship gathering. We noted the excesses of speech (12:1–3) and the irreverent and disgraceful behavior at the meal-rite (11:20–22, 27–34). It is therefore to be expected that Paul will issue *a call to good order, self-control, and a disciplined way of conducting the worship:* No blasphemous outcry, such as "a curse on Jesus" (12:3) emanates from the Holy Spirit's activity. Further, speaking, praying, and praising "with my spirit" is good (14:15, 16), but these exercises must be firmly kept under the control of—as they are complemented by and conjoined to—speaking, praying, and praising "with my mind." "My spirit" is an ambiguous phrase (C. K. Barrett notes the possibilities); it appears to mean "my spiritual gift" that leads to the various exercises; hence I have a responsibility, Paul insists, to employ the gift yet not to abuse its privilege by allowing it to get out of hand and lead me into a trancelike state where I cease to be held accountable for what takes place. The interpretation is supported by (*i*) the way Paul writes somewhat disdainfully of "my mind" as being "unfruitful" (i.e., inactive and not producing any good) when the speaker is exercising a glossolalic gift; (*ii*) the encouragement to *seek* exactly those gifts which serve the church's well-being suggests a Christian's active participation (so plainly in v. 32: "the spirits of the prophets are subject to the control of the prophets"). He or she is responsible to seek the health-producing gifts, and thereby to turn from what is only self-gratifying and maybe destructive of the *koinōnia* of the church; (*iii*) the criterion that a person must calculate what will be the effect on others. If worship gets out of hand, the onlooker will dismiss Christians as people "demon-possessed" (v. 23; not simply "deranged" but positively demonically controlled); and (*iv*) the plain warnings of verse 43: God is not a God of "anarchy" (*akatastasia,* a word otherwise meaning insurrection, Luke 21:9).

The apostle's exhortation stands at the close: let "everything be done in a fitting and orderly way" (14:40).

THE POSITIVE CONTRIBUTION OF PAUL'S TEACHING

From the foregoing—and before we get to the detailed discussion of this chapter—three "principles" to define and regulate Christian worship in a "healthy" church emerge.

(a) There is clearly for Paul the need for *the Spirit's control.* Granting the freedom of the Holy Spirit to inspire both the praying and the praising (vv. 14–16), Paul is careful to insist that worship should not get out of hand (v. 32) and so allow an open door to anarchy. The reason for this warning is given in verse 23: "so if the whole church comes together and everyone speaks in tongues, and some who do not understand [or, some inquirers] or some unbelievers come in, will they not say that you are out of your mind?" This lamentable effect on the outsider is to bring worship into disrepute; on the other side, nonecstatic gifts or ecstatic gifts that promote the building up of the church—and so touch the outsider as a direct consequence—are, in Paul's esteem (as E. Schweizer understands it), "the real yardstick for estimating the value of ministries."[2] Here is a good clue for the exegesis of 14:22 whose "plain" sense is often taken to say the opposite.

(b) As a consequence, what counts above all is *social responsibility in worship*. We do not worship as separate units who "happen" to be in the same place, sitting in adjacent seats or nearby in pews, and singing the same hymns as we go through the motions of worship together. We are there as "one body" (1 Cor. 12:12, 13)—and this oneness is also the Spirit's gift.

E. Schweizer has also written trenchantly of the failure of much modern worship precisely because it does not lead to and so express fellowship-in-worship. He says, "It is completely foreign to the New Testament to split the Christian community into one speaker and a silent body of listeners."[3]

(c) There is a *special ministry* in corporate worship that gives it a dignity and decorum different from our worship as individuals, family members, or even as parts of subgroups in the Christian society. We may concede that what this chapter (1 Cor. 14) depicts is the coming-together of a house congregation (v. 26), yet it must not be overlooked that, for all their divisiveness and cliquishness, the Corinthians *did* unite in a common liturgical meeting (as J. Héring observes),[4] and Paul repeatedly stresses here the idea of "the *entire* church" assembling together.

The fact of "the church of God at Corinth" meeting in one place lends to its worship an importance—and so a style and ethos—that cannot always be true of smaller units of believers when they meet in fellowship, Bible study, prayer, and for the purposes of mutual enrichment, called today "sharing." There is, in a public service, a desired blend of the formal with the intimate that never descends to the level of what is no better than the casual or even flippant, which loses the sense of the majesty and mystery of God whom we adore and the sense of the numinous that both awakens our healthy "awe" and speaks to reassure our salutary fear. So Richard John Neuhaus reminds us:

> Worship is the perilous enactment of God's *sacramentum* with us, and ours with him. When we speak of worship as "celebration," we must know that we are not celebrating our securities and satisfactions. We are celebrating the perilous business of love—of that supreme love that did not and does not turn back from the cross.[5]

For all the apparent features in 1 Corinthians 14 that could be summed up under the heading of spontaneity and freedom, we can cite counterbalancing emphases that caution us against confusing "spontaneity" with "eccentricity," or "familiarity" with "chumminess" (Neuhaus's terms). The upshot of this way of viewing worship is put in simple language that speaks to a pressing modern pastoral problem: with all the stress today on worship as "encounter" (and 1 Cor. 14 is usually the proof-text for such a designation), we need to recall and to hold constantly before us the thought that "worship chiefly has to do not with encountering one another but with encountering God."

PROCLAIMING/PROPHESYING

We are now ready to tackle the three areas where Paul applies these ideas. First, verses 1–12 are devoted to the subject of "prophesying," or as we have suggestively rendered, "proclaiming."

At the close of his tribute to "love" Paul places the expected injunction: "Make love your aim" (lit. "pursue" [*diōkete*] the love I have just been describing, or—if my reconstruction of 13:13b is possible—"set your sights on God's love" in a way parallel to Paul's call in Phil. 3:12, 14: "I pursue the prize of God's call," and [in a negative sense] of Gentiles' not seeking the divine righteousness [as in Rom. 10:3]). At all events, "Pursue love" or even more tellingly "Follow the way of love" goes back to 12:31 and represents the answering call to Paul's earlier promise: "I show you a still better way." Clearly that *is* the path of love, and Paul intends his readers to lay the counsel to heart and practice it in their lives. The first readers needed such an admonition, as we have seen, in the light of the confusion that reigned at Corinth over "spiritual gifts."

Paul's total answer has been in terms of the more excellent *charismata,* which, however, are valueless or worse until they are accompanied and directed by love. *Charismata* is evidently Paul's word and it puts all the emphasis on the divine character (*charis*) of the gifts (*charis-mata*). We have suggested that spirit-gifts (*pneumatika*) is the Corinthians' terminology; they had inquired about these manifestations and sought Paul's ruling (12:1). Interestingly, in chapter 14 *charismata* drops out, and Paul picks up the Corinthians' terms, probably actually citing their statements only to correct them. As M.-A. Chevallier puts it:

> In order to correct on theological grounds the Corinthian idea of pneumatika, Paul has brought in the idea of the charismata, the graces which God gives by his Spirit for the life of the community.[6]

I think there may be two places where this literary device is seen:

(a) "You are striving for *pneumatika*" (as in 12:31a) is a quoted insertion from the readers' own position, since both the verb (*zēloute*) and noun, as we observed, reflect their ambition. Paul quickly modifies the statement with an adversative, "but rather (*mallon*) that you may prophesy." Chevallier gives a special value to Paul's word "but" (*de*), which plays the part, he submits, of an ordinal number: "first, love: and *then* the *pneumatika*." He is using the criterion of what is excellent to set the *pneumatika* in their rightful order; but as Conzelmann notes, the test is no longer that of *agapē*, it is *oikodomē*, that which builds up the community life. *Oikodomē* is thus the chapter's keyword (Senft).

(b) At 14:12 we are actually told that this was the Corinthians' position: "So it is even with you: since you are eager to have spirit-gifts" (*pneumata*). Paul quotes this concession but proceeds straightway to revise it: "try to *excel* in gifts that build up the church" ("excel" is *perisseuēte*, a verb that suggests that which is gained as an enrichment [1 Cor. 8:8], and may reflect Paul's comment on the Corinthians' watchword, "it is for our best" [1 Cor. 6:12; 10:23]). What Paul thought of as being for the church's chief good is their "upbuilding"; and how he conceived that desired end to be reached is contained in 14:1–25.

So he highlights "prophesying" (14:3), a spirit-gift that aims to bring God's truth to bear on human lives with a view to their *understanding* and *growth*. He sets the gift of *prophēteia* over against "tongues" in four ways, outlined by John Goldingay,[7] which we may indicate with some modifications:

(a) Tongues cannot be directly understood by human beings, whereas prophecy can (14:2–3a, 7–11). In glossolalia, at least in this section where Paul seems to refer to the use of tongues in private devotion when the communion of an individual with God is so intimate and profound that no earthly language can be the vehicle of its expression (cf. Rom. 8:26, 27; 2 Cor. 12:2–4), the speaker in a rapture utters words that are not immediately intelligible. "The glossolalist speaks *to* God rather than *from* God."[8] "Communion" with God is of the essence of the experience, rather than "communication" with God, a term otherwise preferred by J. D. G. Dunn.[9]

In prophecy, however, there is no such barrier to instant communication: "the prophet, although inspired, speaks in a comprehensible language and, without interpretation, can have a beneficial effect on the meeting," J. Héring remarks.[10] The exact nature of this type of public speaking is spelled out in verse 3: it is a ministry that builds up, and exhorts, and comforts. These verbs offer a thumbnail sketch of the role of "prophets" in the Pauline communities; the essence of the prophetic ministry is its immediate intelligibility, and its resultant capability of speaking a word "to the situation of need in the assembly" (J. D. G. Dunn, who remarks that the distinguishing mark of prophecy over against glossolalia is not inspiration but intelligibility).[11] Paul gives three illustrations to contrast ecstatic "tongues" with inspired "prophecy": (*i*) from ancient musical practices (v. 7); (*ii*) from military parades (v. 8); and (*iii*) from simple conversation that can only be carried on effectively if the speakers understand each other (vv. 9–11). Flute and harp give different sounds to make harmony and melody; the trumpet blast sounds to call the troops to battle (Judg. 7:19–23) and demands a response; human speech is meaningful as it communicates the thoughts of the speakers. In all, the point of the analogy is the same, though we may pinpoint the nature of various responses as (*i*) *pleasure,* when music is harmonious (Mozart's *Musical Joke,* K.522, is the exception to prove the rule); (*ii*) *obedience,* as the army gets the signal to advance; (*iii*) *satisfaction,* as a person derives fulfillment from both speaking to a friend and hearing the friend's conversation. There are sounds that take on meaning as they make sense. So it is with Christian speaking: unless the hearers catch the drift of what is being said and understand it, they will dismiss such noises as those of a "gibberish talker" (Conzelmann) whose words seem none other than "barbar" (*barbaros,* v. 11). And that is both a waste of time and a travesty of the worship situation where "words" should convey meaningful truth.

(b) Tongues benefit the speaker, while prophecy serves to benefit the whole company (vv. 3b–6, 12). We should not minimize, as Paul grants, the way "tongues" do fulfill a role in private worship. W. J. Hollenweger[12] notes that "tongues speaking" is evidently of two types: "hot," that is, involving ecstatic utterances that can easily border on frenzy and unrestrained outbursts (as in 12:1–3 perhaps); and what he calls "cool," a more mystical experience that can readily be controlled, a point derived from 14:28 where we read that Paul expected a glossolalic to be able to keep his or her utterance under restraint. Evidently Paul's own use of glossolalia was of the second type (14:18) and his advocacy "do not forbid speaking in tongues" (14:39) is in regard to the same species of glossolalia. And we may appeal to 12:30, Paul's emphatic declaration that "not all speak in tongues," as being explained by this distinction he makes between "tongues" that are acceptable (14:5, 13, with the necessary qualification) and those that are not, since the latter type promotes only confusion (14:23) and must not be given free rein—certainly not among the excitable Corinthians who were (apparently) also falling into theological error by treating "tongues of angels" (13:1) as a proof of their realized eschatology, with its promise of a celestial life already begun on earth.

Prophecy, on the contrary, has no such attendant risks. It is above all "a sign for believers" (14:22). The exercise of this gift plays a multifaceted role, as Paul understood it (the list is one of intelligible gifts, all virtually synonymous with prophecy; so Barrett). Primarily it "builds up" the congregation so that it can function as a mature body of Christ (14:5, 12). The verbs in 14:3 tell us as much. There is equally another side to prophecy. It confirms believers in the faith they profess, and in particular it imparts a peculiar form of "God-consciousness" as the divine presence is known in such a dramatic way that even the unbeliever or casual visitor to the assembly is immediately struck with holy fear and forced to acknowledge that "God is really among you" (vv. 24, 25). J. D. G. Dunn draws the extended conclusion from this scene that "prophecy edifies because it does not exalt man but humbles him, making him aware that he stands before God in all his vulnerability."[13] Just how this is accomplished, on the human level, is difficult to say. Evidently the prophets' words were charged with a "numinous" power that pierced the shell of complacency; and possibly, with Käsemann, we should see this "unmasking" of the unbeliever as effected by the uttering of the so-called "sentences of holy law" (e.g., 1 Cor. 3:17; 14:38; 16:22a) of the order "destruction to the destroyer"—except that these words were first directed to the professed believers as a rebuke and overheard by the outsider.[14] The judgment that came on Ananias and Sapphira (Acts 5:11) may be seen as an example of this, since as a result, we are told, "great fear seized the whole church *and all who heard about these events*" (v. 11).

PRAYING

(c) This section demands a separate heading since it is concerned not so much with prophesying as with praying (14:13–15). The gist of Paul's treatment is that whereas the exercise of "tongues" involves the Spirit, both to impart the glossolalic gift and to enable that utterance to be interpreted (whether by himself or by another [v. 27]), there is a type of praying that is *both* "in the Spirit" *and* "with the mind"—a description that exactly fits the prophetic ministry that "speaks . . . intelligible [lit. "with my mind"] words" (v. 19).

Paul touches here on what we may call, in modern terms, the psychology of prayer. "If I pray in a tongue, my spirit prays"—or perhaps "the Spirit in me," referring to the work of the Holy Spirit within the believer (C. K. Barrett considers the various options in interpreting a cryptic phrase, *to pneuma mou*)—"but my mind is *unfruitful*" (v. 14). The last word implies that the human intellect in this kind of ecstatic praying lies dormant, contributing nothing to the process of articulating thoughts into words. Here is perhaps the central place where Paul tells us what he believes glossolalia to be. It suggests an enraptured fellowship with God when the human spirit is in such deep, hidden communion with the divine Spirit that "words"—at best broken utterances of our secret selves —are formed by a spiritual upsurge requiring no mental effort.

His next phrase is slightly enigmatic: *ti oun estin*—"What then is it?" C. K. Barrett renders: What is to be done then? suggesting a state of affairs needing to be put right. "If I pray in a tongue, part, and that a most significant part, of my nature remains out of action. This is not good for me, and it is not good for the community I ought to serve." So Paul proceeds to qualify the use of glossolalia: "I will pray with the spirit [the personal pronoun is dropped, as Barrett notes, but most translators retain it], but [*de*] I will pray with the mind also [*kai*]." These two qualifications, at first sight insignificant, are important: one sets up a contrast ("but . . .") and the other adds another component that Paul deemed vital to a proper understanding of prayer. Rational prayer takes precedence over irrational utterances, especially in the congregational assembly. The reason is not far to seek. It lies in the effect on the outsider, as we have seen (vv. 23–25); and "strange sounds" have a detrimental consequence on interested non-Christians who visit the Corinthians at their worship.

The upshot of Paul's discussion is to do two things: (*i*) to curtail the use of tongues to private praying presumably at home (14:28: "let him speak *to himself*"), when no interpreter seemingly is needed. The glossolalic "utters mysteries with his spirit" (or "in the Spirit," v. 2) and "builds himself up"—a verb that suggests to M. E. Thrall[15] a note of condemnation or at least disdain of this practice: "to regard it [glossolalia] as the gift supremely to be desired is a form of selfishness," because it forgets the ever-insistent need for the *charismata* to build up the church or "the other person" (v. 17) who may overhear my "private" communion. More likely what Paul is opposing is an understanding of worship as a private exercise in which individuals seal themselves off from others and concentrate exclusively on their own personal experiences.

Paul therefore wants (*ii*) to insist on "interpretation" when "tongues" occur in the assembly, precisely to guard against this. For him worship takes on its true character when it is corporate, or at least expressed in a way that is related to the growth and enrichment of the entire body. His purpose is probably polemical, namely, in resisting the notion of the "church" as a Gnostic conventicle made up of persons each with his or her own privatized religious exercises and ambitions.

PRAISING

All that Paul said about "praying" in spirit and with the mind is repeated and applied in reference to the offering of praise (v. 15). The vehicle of praise is a type of singing, "a kind of *charismatic hymnody*" (J. D. G. Dunn's phrase)[16] that includes both singing in tongues and singing with intelligible words. The setting of this verse is difficult to pinpoint and it is just as uncertain whether Paul has in mind singing that is spontaneous or the use of a precomposed "hymn," which seems required at 14:26 since a person brings such a composition to the meeting. The evidence for charismatic singing is seen elsewhere, such as in Ephesians 5:18f.: "Do not get drunk with wine . . . be filled with the Spirit. Speak to one another with psalms, hymns, and spiritual songs. Sing and make music in your heart to the Lord." In the parallel text of

Colossians 3:16 the use of "spiritual songs," that is, songs inspired by the Spirit, is set in a context of the didactic ministry ("the word of Christ . . . teach . . . counsel one another with all wisdom"), though I suggest that this emphasis denotes a shift from the Corinthian scene with its acceptance of a more spontaneous, unstructured format of worship (even in 14:26, which Paul is probably reporting and seeking to correct, as we shall see later). The singing at Corinth may have been expressed in enraptured cries or acclamations (not always acceptable to Paul, as we see from 1 Cor. 12:3). Yet the stress on "thanksgiving" in 14:16 and 17 suggests a more extended type of praise, perhaps borrowed from the Jewish *hôdāyāh* ("I thank thee") form.

Even such a personal aspect of worship as this "singing in the Spirit" has to be safeguarded, according to Paul. What is offered in song is intended to be "understood" (v. 16) even by an ordinary person, who is here presumably to be equated with an "inquirer" whose Christian status is not yet accepted but who is a "catechumen" (like Theophilus, Luke 1:4?). That person must be able to know what is being said or sung so that he or she may respond with the affirmation, "Amen," to the thanksgiving.

The inference here is that Paul expected Christian praise to be meaningful and not simply—as it seems to have been at Corinth—the effusion of emotional, subrational outbursts, whether in an ecstasy of joy or in the releasing of pent-up feelings in shouts of nonsense syllables, or "primal numinous sounds" vocalizing the collective memory of a group (Williams). [17] Paul's allusion to "five intelligible words" spoken to build up the church (v. 18) qualifies his concession that he, too, knew the gift of glossolalia, presumably in his "mystical" experiences such as the one recorded in 2 Corinthians 12 (Conzelmann); or it may be his argument *ad hominem*, conceding the phenomenon of "tongues" at Corinth for the sake of making a corrective point. It is noteworthy, as Cyril G. Williams points out, [18] that in the New Testament "there is no concrete evidence of glossolalia," that is, no glossolalic speech is reported as such. The call to adult maturity in "thinking" is to offset the "childish" practice of tongues-speaking (perhaps a reference back to 13:11, "when I was an infant [*nēpios*, lit. "not able to speak"], I spoke [*elaloun*; the verb *lalein* means to speak in a tongue in this Corinthian context, says M.-A. Chevallier] [19] like an in-

fant"). At all events, the apostle's conclusion in verse 20 stands out
clearly: "do not be children [*paidia*] in your thinking . . . but in
your thinking be mature [*teleioi*]."

(d) The next section (vv. 21–25) is especially difficult to ex-
egete. Its plain teaching—if verse 22 is central—is that "tongues"
are less desirable than "prophecy" because they affect "unbelievers" in quite different ways, and Paul has in his mind's eye a
situation where the "unbelievers" (*apistoi*) are present in the congregational worship.

Paul recalls to his readers the Old Testament passage (Isa.
28:11, 12) in which Yahweh threatens to punish his rebellious
people Israel by foreign invaders (in this case the Assyrians) whose
strange language will mystify the Jewish nation (cf. Isa. 36:11ff.).
Because the Jewish kingdom remained obstinate to the prophet's
warning and pleading in God's name, they would be judged by (*i*)
suffering a foreign invasion and (*ii*) being hardened in their unbelief (Isa. 6:9–13). In the Old Testament context these strange
"tongues," spoken by the Assyrian enemies, confirmed unbelieving Israel in their unbelief and so acted deleteriously.

Paul now takes over this reference to Isaiah 28, which, I suggest, is found not only in the cited text of verse 21 but also in verse
22 where he offers a midrash (interpretative comment) on the Old
Testament quotation. The midrash on "men of strange tongues"/
"lips of foreigners" applies the effect of speech on the unbelieving
people of Israel; this midrashic application is then related to Isaiah's "prophecy" (in v. 22), which has a good effect. "Tongues" is
taken in its Old Testament sense of Assyrian (foreign) languages,
which confirmed (by God's judgment) Israel's apostasy, whereas
Isaiah's prophetic ministry was beneficial to the remnant of Israel
that believed (Isa. 8:16). We can observe a precedent for this
Pauline use of the Old Testament[20] in 2 Corinthians 3:16 and 17
and Philippians 2:15 (the reference to ethnic Israel as a "crooked
and depraved generation" becomes in Paul's hands a transferred—
or midrashic—allusion to the pagan world around the Israel of the
church). The novelty of this way of exegeting 1 Corinthians 14:21
and 22 is to remove the references to "tongues" and "prophecy"
from the Corinthian scene, whereas, as the references stand they
appear to say exactly the opposite of what Paul elsewhere in this
chapter intends. *His* position is, rather: "tongues" build up believers, albeit in a private capacity (14:2, 4), and "prophecy"

builds up the church, but also has a signal and salutary effect on the nonbeliever (14:23–25).

Alternatively, granting now that verse 22 has the Corinthian problems in view, we may stress Paul's use of "signs." That term (*sēmeion*) is understood by some commentators in the sense of what the charismatic gift is intended to do, rather than as a witness to what is already a fact. We may also point, with J. Héring, to the present participles used: "those coming to faith" (*tois pisteuousin*) in the two places where verse 22 in translation normally reads "believers." Then the sense will be:

> Ecstatic utterance (tongues) is not intended to be something which produces belief in Christianity. It is a phenomenon which leaves non-Christians in their unbelieving state. Prophecy, on the other hand, is intended not to confirm unbelievers in their unbelief, but to encourage conversion to the Christian faith.[21]

The net effect is to praise the superiority of "prophecy," which is a sign "in the sense that it produces believers," that is, those coming to faith (cf. Bruce). "Tongues," on the contrary, serves[22] only to alienate strangers and lead to the travestied conclusion that "madness" (demonic possession) reigns in the Christian assembly.

The apostle's concern is for believers to speak the prophetic word that, even if not directly aimed at "unbelievers" (cf. 14:3), will have a salutary operation. E. Schweizer finds here a litmus test of authentic worship, namely, the impression it leaves on the "outsider" or casual visitor as well as the value it promotes in helping believers and catechumens.[23]

Verse 25 is one of the most dramatic descriptions of early Christian worship we have. "Prophecy" carries a judgment-power. Whether it acts on the Corinthians as professed believers (who evidently were demeaning its role and shutting their ears to such prophets as exposed their failings like ancient Israel sadly apostate; hence they were incurring divine displeasure, as in 10:1–22; 11:34) or on real "unbelievers" who "drop in" to view the service of worship, the consequence is the same. "Prophecy" acts as a divine judgment, revealing a person's secret thoughts and confronting him with the truth that humbles and saves. His prostration (as an act of obeisance in Gen. 17:3; Luke 5:12; Rev. 7:11; 11:16, a creaturely awareness of frailty in the presence of the numinous) and his acknowledgment that "God is really among you" are, in the text, of the essence of true "worship" (*proskynēsis,* parallel with the OT picture of worship as "bowing down," the verbal *hištaḥᵃwāh*).

The key phrase is "God is *truly among you*" (*ontōs . . . en hymin*). Clearly *en* cannot mean "in" you, for that would be exactly what the Gnostic Corinthians would hold as true of themselves as "men and women of the spirit" (*hoi pneumatikoi,* imbued with *pneuma*). The total phrase is taken, not from 1 Kings 18:39 (as some suggest) but from Isaiah 45:14, or more tellingly Zechariah 8:23: "Let us go with you, for we have heard that God is with you." In other words, what was predicted of the end time, namely, the turning of the Gentiles to Israel in an acknowledgment that Israel's God was "truly" to be found among his people, is now a present reality. Worship, for Paul, shares that eschatological quality of confronting the gathered company with the divine presence in such a way that what is fervently hoped for as the final victory of God's reign is already shared, at least in part and as a token, in the present as an experienced reality.[24]

In this light we are perhaps meant to read Paul's concluding statement, buttressed by scriptural citation, as a polemical counterposition to what was being urged at Corinth. In their enthusiasm and preference for the more individualistic spirit-gifts (*pneumatika*), some Corinthians were claiming that *their* type of worship brought the future into the present. Paul retorts by partly agreeing that in worship we do glimpse and experience heavenly realities ("God is really here"), though never to the exclusion of the fullness of worship reserved for the future fulfillment of eschatological hope. Our worship, as our knowledge, is "in part" (1 Cor. 13:12). Yet, Paul goes on, what we do have now is that expression and experience of worship that brings us face to face, not with *our* spiritual ecstasies and emotional exaltation, but with God before whom the most fitting posture is to bow down and confess that he, by his Spirit, reads our secret thoughts and convicts us of our frail humanity and utter dependence on him. It is the function of the *charismata,* properly exercised in love and with an eye on the needs of the community, to lead worshipers to that goal.

Translation

26–33   *What follows therefore,*[a] brethren? When you assemble together, each one of you *has*[b] a psalm, or a teaching, or a revelation, or a tongue, or an interpretation. [Fine!] *Let all* (contributions) *be for upbuilding.*[c]

If anyone speaks in a tongue, let two or at most three speak, and in turn, and let one person interpret. If there is no interpreter, let the speaking be *private*[d] and to God. As for prophets, let two or three speak, and let the *others*[e] judge. If a revelation comes to another who is seated, let the first one be silent. For all of you have the opportunity to prophesy one by one, that all may be encouraged. The spirits of the prophets are under the control of the prophets; for God is not a God of disorder but of harmony.

34–36   As *in all the congregations of God's people,*[f] let your women keep silent in the congregations, for they are not allowed to speak. Rather let them be *under control,*[g] just as *the ruling says.*[h] If they wish to learn anything, let them ask *their own husbands*[i] at home, for it is shameful for a woman *to speak*[j] in the congregation. Was it from you that God's message went out? Did it reach you alone?

37–40   If any person thinks that he or she is a prophet or a spirit-possessed person, let that one know that *what I write* to you[k] is from the Lord. If anyone ignores it (my ruling), he is to be ignored. So then, my brothers, *"you are striving to prophesy and you are not forbidding speaking in tongues"*[l] [Good]; let everything (you do) be done in a seemly manner and in good order.

Points to Ponder

a. τί οὖν ἐστιν; : lit. "What then is it?" Paul sums up the situation.

b. Note the repetition of ἔχει, "has," as if to stress the individual contributions.

c. A Pauline corrective comment, I think. See my essay, "Some Reflections on NT Hymns" in *Christ the Lord. Studies in Christology presented to Donald Guthrie,* ed. H. H. Rowdon (1982), 37–49.

d. ἑαυτῷ, "to himself" (v. 2). Conzelmann renders (correctly if in a paraphrase) "at home"; cf. 14:35.

e. "Others." Who are they? Leaders? Church members? Other prophets?

f. A notorious textual *crux*: Where does the phrase belong? My translation keeps it in verse 34, but there is some tautology involved. Maybe this is Paul's emphasis as it was needed.

The verses that follow are also textually suspect; see G. Zuntz, *The Text of the Epistles* (1953), 17, and E. E. Ellis in B. M. Metzger Festschrift volume, *New Testament Textual Criticism,* ed. E. J. Epp and G. D. Fee (1980), 213–20.

g. Matching ὑποτασσέσθωσαν with ὑποτάσσεται in verse 32.

h. νόμος is of course "the Law" (of Moses, or Torah); but where is the appropriate text in the OT? Hence my rendering, based on the sense of *nomos* = norm, principle (Rom. 3:27; Gal. 6:2).

i. τοὺς ἰδίους ἄνδρας (though it is a set-phrase in the station codes: Eph. 5:22; 1 Pet. 3:1) connects with γυναῖκες (v. 34) where the addition ὑμῶν ("*your* womenfolk") seems to point to women leaders in the congregation, as in 1 Timothy 3:11 and more particularly 1 Timothy 2:11–15. The "silencing" of the women in the Pastorals and the forbidding ("I do not allow a woman to teach") both suggest a wrongful aspiration to the teaching office which at Ephesus had led the women into heterodox opinions (cf. 1 Tim. 5:11–15). The enigmatic promise in 1 Timothy 2:15: "she will be saved through child-bearing" if they (presumably wives and husbands) continue in faith, etc. will then relate to deliverance from the danger of being branded a false teacher, as suggested by S. Jebb, *The Expository Times* 81 (1969–70):221f. and developed by Mark D. Roberts, "Woman shall be saved: A closer look at 1 Timothy 2:15," *Theological Students' Fellowship Bulletin* 5.2 (Nov. 1981):4–7. He refers to an innovative contribution by Richard and Catherine Clark Kroeger, "May Women Teach? Heresy in the Pastoral Epistles," *Reformed Journal* 30 (Oct. 1980):14–18.

Dennis R. MacDonald, *The Legend and the Apostle* (1983), ch. 3, has reopened the question but he plays down the role of the Ephesian women as purveyors of un-Pauline teaching by making their cardinal error one of preferring celibacy over the married state (but see 1 Tim. 4:3).

j. Notice λαλεῖν, "to speak" ecstatically.

k. ἃ γράφω would support my view in h.

l. A self-defensive Corinthian statement, I submit, which Paul accepts but only with modification in verse 40.

CHAPTER FIVE

MEN AND WOMEN
AT WORSHIP

INTRODUCTION

The section that begins at 1 Corinthians 14:26 picks up and carries forward Paul's earlier discussion on the church's activity in assembling for united praise, praying, and proclamation. It is just as evident that he is addressing some prevalent needs at Corinth whose churchly ethos is seen above all at 14:12. Paul grants that they are "eager for spirits" (i.e., "spiritual gifts," presumably the Corinthians' catchphrase). We have noted Paul's concern to interject some controls to regulate such an "ambition" that evidently led to a misplaced evaluation of pneumatic phenomena, particularly glossolalia and the gift of *gnōsis*. The Corinthians were divided over these very issues; and it is likely we can overhear the claims of the self-styled "spiritual persons" (*hoi pneumatikoi,* mentioned by inference in 14:37) in Paul's rebuttal of those who prized "knowledge" and "wisdom" (1 Cor. 1:7—4:21).[1] The trait that merits his sternest rebuke is seen in 1 Corinthians 8:1: "*gnōsis* puffs up," whereas (he goes on) "love (*agapē*) builds up." The dissension and strife that characterized the Corinthian assembly are very much in the apostle's mind as he addresses the actual conduct of worship. The lead-in comes at verse 26:

> What follows then, brothers? [from the previous discussion that concludes by setting inspired "prophecy" at the heart of the congregational worship]. When you assemble, each of you has a psalm, or a teaching, or a revelation, or a tongue, or an interpretation: let everything be done for building up.

It is not clear whether the description of the worship service is just that: a reporting by Paul of what he expected to happen, which he accepts only to regulate quickly by his remark that whatever item is contributed, it should lead to the upbuilding of all concerned (Robertson-Plummer[2] take the meaning thus: Paul says everyone has, *not* everyone has to have; it would be strengthened if the introducing phrase, *ti oun estin,* were taken in a different sense ["What does this imply?"], looking back to the situation of v. 23 and finding fault with that scene where "tongues" are out of hand). At all events, Paul's argument will lead to the ultimate conclusion that stresses the importance of *"good* order" which alone can build up the body.

PAULINE ORDER

It may be well to set down the three principles that govern this section as far as it relates to congregational worship.

(a) *Paul holds the entire church constantly in his sights* throughout this debate and as his counterposition to the Corinthian enthusiasts who were far more interested in private religious experiences. The enumeration of the various contributions to worship in verse 26 with the verb repeated five times ("each one *has*") may be intended to hold up the Corinthian individualism to reproof. Evidently each person was parading his or her own gift as a prized possession and regarding that as all-important. The Pauline response is to stress *oikodomē,* which is for Paul a corporate exercise. Hence, Paul bids the glossolalic who cannot *share* his message with the whole company to keep silent and restrict the use of the "tongue" to his private surroundings (v. 28) as part of his fellowship alone with God (14:2, 4; Paul grants that he may "build up" himself, but this effect is immediately offset by the larger concern a person *should* have, as in 14:39).

The same type of restriction on the "tongues"-speaker is seen in the rule laid down for the exercise of that gift. Not only is the interpreter's work essential for the proper use of the "tongue" in public assembly; the number of those offering such revelations is strictly limited to two speakers "or at most three, and each in turn," to be followed by the interpretation of each in order, with evidently one person charged with the role of interpreter ("let one person [*heis*] interpret," v. 27, though 12:10 mentions "the interpretation of tongues" as a gift accorded to members in a general way. It has been proposed that the glossolalia could do his or her own interpreting on the ground that "let one interpret" looks back to 14:13.[3] V. 28a *could* be rendered as by Weiss: "But if he is not an interpreter. . ."). The strict control of the glossolalia is designed to keep it in check lest it become an unruly outburst, leading to the confusion described in verses 23 and 24.

(b) *Paul turns his mind to "prophecy" with the same consideration in view.* That gift too must be exercised in an orderly fashion. While the ban on the number of the prophets, which limited the glossolalics to a maximum of three, "by turns," is not repeated—the phrase *to pleiston,* "at most," is omitted in verse 29, and in verse 31 "all of you . . . one by one" are encouraged to prophesy—it still remains that Paul wishes to impose some controls on the prophetic ministry, even if he regards it highly.

Prophets who bring a message are liable to have their utterances tested (14:29: "let the others judge" [*diakrinetōsan*]). Before we look at this ministry of "discernment" that is to accompany the prophets' function in the church, we must review how Paul understood this "gift of prophecy." David Hill[4] has isolated several conclusions that seem very well established: (*i*) At Corinth there was a fairly well-defined circle of "prophets" (1 Cor. 12:28; 14:29ff.; cf. Rom. 12:8 for their presence in other congregations). (*ii*) The call to prophesy was a general one, inviting all to share in this ministry (14:5, 24 ["everyone is prophesying"], 31 ["you can all prophesy in turn" *or* "all of you have the opportunity to prophesy one by one"]), though Paul does impose a limit in verse 29, in the interests of time (Barrett) or more probably good order. Yet we should not overlook 12:29: "Are all prophets?" with its expected answer, "No." (*iii*) The prophets exercised a key role in the building up of the community (14:4b), and he or she (1 Cor. 11:5) does this in terms of the type of utterance (intelligible speaking) and its content (14:3).[5] (*iv*) Yet "prophecy" is partial and temporary as a *charisma*; its usefulness will cease when the consummation comes, presumably at the parousia of Christ (13:9, 10). (*v*) In the meanwhile Paul placed great emphasis on this part of public worship where "prophecy" finds its natural ambience and setting in the life of the church.

In addition we may note the following. "Prophecy" aims at instructing others (14:19) and leading them to a deeper apprehension of God's will for his people. Hill defines this in terms of "pastoral exhortation" (14:3; *paraklēsis*), which is a term in partnership with "upbuilding" and "comfort" (*paramythia*). All these ideas are grounded in the gospel in that the prophet's message "constantly refers back to the work of salvation as its presupposition and basis";[6] hence prophecy can promote evangelistic purposes and lead to an outsider's conviction and conversion. The twice-repeated "by all" (*hypo pantōn*; v. 24) lends some credence to J. Héring's suggestion[7] that, as "all" seems most naturally to relate to the prophets in their messages, what they have is a gift of thought reading or discretion to speak the "right" word calculated to bring the visitor to a realization of his or her need as a sinner (cf. NIV). But the aim of the prophets is *not primarily* evangelism: they speak to "instruct," and their hearers are in their presence to "learn" (v. 31; cf. v. 35).

The clinching argument in support of this last point is that the prophets' speeches are subject to testing. This clearly shows that the matters under discussion are exactly that: under discussion by everyone present. Prophecy, therefore, is not an evangelistic ministry whose message remains an imperious call to obedience without question (see Rom. 10:8–15 for a clear statement of how Paul viewed the Christian proclamation of the kerygma). The response to the kerygma is the "obedience of faith" (Rom. 1:5; cf. Gal. 3:5); the response to *prophēteia* is the exercise of the gift labeled *diakrisis*—evaluating, discerning, assessing, testing the oracles that are the offerings of the prophets.

But what is this "testing," and who is to be responsible for such activity of *diakrisis*? Since the prophets' ministry is by definition one in intelligible speech, the verb *diakrinō* cannot be taken in one of its otherwise legitimate senses of "explain" or "interpret." U. B. Müller[8] logically deduces that, since prophecy is conveyed in intelligible words, there is surely no need to have those utterances "explained." It follows that "prophecy" is subject to scrutiny in the sense of its utterance being weighed and tested to see if it is in accord with the "mind of the Spirit"—a phrase derived from Romans 8:27, but 1 Corinthians 2:16 speaks of "the mind of the Lord" in a context (1 Cor. 2:10–16) that suggests spiritual discernment. This fact may explain Paul's phrase in 12:10, *diakrisis pneumatōn*, a testing of prophetic spirits, which refers as much to the source as to the substance of what constituted the prophetic oracle. Obviously a blasphemous cry like "Jesus be damned!" in 12:3 stands self-condemned; it does not emanate from the Holy Spirit, but shows the presence of some alien spirit. The true gift of "prophecy" stands within the orbit of the lordship of Christ, as confessed in hymnic speech as well as practiced in personal life (see *Didache* 11:8: "Not everyone making ecstatic utterances is a prophet, but only if he behaves like the Lord"). Above all, the prophet's words serve to upbuild the congregation (one instance, still ambiguous, is seen in *Didache* 11:11 where the "genuine prophet . . . acts with a view to symbolizing the mystery of the Church"). For Paul the chief stress falls on "instructing others" (14:19) who become "learners" (14:31), as we saw.

How the persons do the "testing" is unclear.[9] Some process of "sifting out," discriminating the good from the spurious, is implied in 1 Thessalonians 5:19–22, *Didache* 11:11, and 1 John 4:1 (here the test is christological soundness). Paul knows that evil prophets are already on the scene (2 Thess. 2:2), just as in Asia Minor there would appear false prophetesses such as "Jezebel" (Rev. 2:20; cf. Mark 13:22 par.). At Corinth there is as yet no sign of intruding false prophets (but by the time Paul wrote 2 Corinthians he was apprehensive of this danger; see 2 Cor. 10–13). The point at issue is rather the content of the oracles that characterize Corinthian worship. Hence the summons is to "investigate" in the sense of weighing the message given to see if it is helpful in "instructing and encouraging" the assembly (14:31).

Two factors are involved here. "The others" (*hoi alloi*) are charged with this responsibility. We may dismiss the idea of a church hierarchy deputed to act as arbiters in this matter (Allo). More debatable, however, is whether the "others" refers to "other prophets" (Conzelmann, Friedrich, Hill, Aune)[10] or to "other church members" present and listening to these utterances (Barrett, Bruce, Dunn).[11] If verse 31 suggests that the prophetic ministry was a widespread phenomenon at Corinth, as is implied by the concentration on "all of you" on whom the Spirit comes, then the two groups may be nearly coextensive (in spite of 12:29). We see the second caution in the scene dramatized in 14:30: "And if a revelation comes to someone who is sitting down" (i.e., not speaking; evidently people *stood* to prophesy), the first speaker (who has begun to prophesy and is on his feet) should stop, that is, keep silence, to permit the person enlightened with a "revelation" (14:6, 26) to give it. Here a definite sequence is in view, which suggests a sensitivity to the Spirit's control and guidance, all in the interests of "good order" and seemly conduct. The confusion that would result from two or more persons speaking simultaneously is averted, leading Paul to his final reminder.

(c) *The need for "order" is paramount* in a situation where pandemonium could break out at any time. Paul detects several possible causes: glossolalics vying with one another and creating a bad impression on the outsider; glossolalics who do not have their esoteric messages interpreted and so "speak into the air" (14:9); a successive line of glossolalics who take up all the time and allow no space to other items of worship (as in the list in v. 26); prophets who speak but permit no "testing" of their oracles; and finally (we will look later at still one more fruitful cause of anarchy, having to do with women prophets) when due precedence is not given to an "apocalyptist" (v. 30) who brings a revelation (*apokalypsis*). Paul's solution seems predicated on certain assumptions. We take them in the order he follows.

(*i*) The prophetic spirit is—and remains at all times—under the prophets' control (v. 32). The verb (*hypotassetai*) is a firm reminder of this: "subject to" is a timely protest against all worship patterns and practices that get "out of hand" and allow the worshipers to be borne along in a frenzy (like in 12:1–3) or in a torrent of irrational utterances that breed only bewilderment and a suspicion of "madness."[12] The noetic character of "prophecy," albeit as a charismatic gift, places a restraint on uncontrolled worship. Such control is evidently lifted in the case of the person with "a revelation" who may not have the ability to contain his message—perhaps because like Agabus or the daughters of Philip he believes he has a *direct* "word of the Lord," or perhaps as a "sentence of holy law" that presses irresistibly through his spirit it must find immediate vocal expression. This priority would account for Paul's accommodation, even to the silencing of the prophet who, offering a *derivative message,* must give way to the apocalyptist and recognize the primacy of the latter. I suggest this is Paul's own position—as apostle and apocalyptic speaker—in verses 37 and 38.

(*ii*) "Order" is what the nature of God dictates. He is not a God of disorder (*akatastasia*: a strong term for a breakdown of order and the onset of chaos and confusion); he is the God "of peace" (perhaps in the Hebrew sense of *shalom,* "wholeness," "integrity," or better, "harmony," a link with 12:24, 25). When every part functions aright and knows its true place, then there is "peace"; when the church members act with respect to the well-being of the community and "strive to excel" in the "greater gifts" that "build up" the congregation, then God is pleased to be there. This is authentic "worship" (14:25)—at Corinth as in all the Pauline congregations (14:33b)—if that is how the phrase is to be construed.

Paul returns to this idealized pattern in verses 39 and 40. He grants that "private" revelations can only be allowed if they contribute to the well-being of the whole. Ecstatic praying (v. 27) is recognized, but controlled and demoted to a lower level than "prophesying." Setting the two *charismata* side by side can be wrongly understood. Notice how the order is inverted: "be eager to prophesy" (recalling and maybe echoing the Corinthians' eagerness in 14:12) *precedes* the tongues, which are "not to be forbidden" (perhaps the Corinthians' own self-justification), an order different from 14:2–5. Also, as Robertson-Plummer observe, there is between these two gifts "a vast difference; the one gift to be greatly longed for, the other only not forbidden."[13]

Paul's parting shot is to express in summary fashion the drift of the entire section: "let everything [done in worship] be in a seemly [*euschēmonōs*, reversing 13:5: "love does not act improperly" (*aschēmonei*)] and orderly [*kata taxin*] way." The "order" (*taxis*) may simply refer to the spirit of worship, that is, without a breakdown of control and self-restraint. Or else the adverb looks back to 14:26 where the "items" in the assembly suggest their relative value in Paul's eyes: first praise (*psalmos*, a hymn addressed to God as in vv. 15, 16), then instruction (by prophecy), third "revelation" (picked up in the permission given in 14:30), and last on the list "tongues" and their needful "interpretation" (cf. 1 Clem. 40 for another usage of *taxis*).

WOMEN AT WORSHIP

Women members at Corinth have already been mentioned at 1 Corinthians 11:5ff. in connection with their role in acting as "prophets," where Paul grants them their "authority" to pray and prophesy. Thus, most commentators experience a difficulty when they have to deal with the section in 14:33b (34)–36 that seemingly denies to women the role Paul had freely granted earlier in the letter.

As in all the congregations of the saints [it could be objected that this phrase goes better with verse 33b and is unnecessarily repeated in the following verse. But that repetition may be exactly Paul's point], let *your* women [or wives, whose husbands are specifically mentioned later] keep silence in the congregations, i.e., *your* assemblies. For they are not permitted to speak, but to be in subjection, as the law also says. If they wish to learn anything, let them ask their own husbands at home, for it is shameful for a woman/wife to speak in church. Was it from you that God's word went out? Did it come to you alone?

This pericope poses problems of several kinds. In order to achieve some harmony between 11:5 and what this restriction seems on face value to impose it has been suggested (*i*) that the task is impossible and Paul is inconsistent or, as Koenig[14] phrases it more delicately, is content with "an unresolved tension in [his] thought"; (*ii*) that the two chapters relate to two quite different contexts; for example, in chapter 11 the situation refers to small, informal gatherings whereas in chapter 14 Paul has in view meetings for the entire church; (*iii*) that the verses are out of place, either as a Pauline fragment out of context, or a deutero-Pauline addition deliberately slipped in by a later editor who sought to bring Paul's teaching into line with the "household code" teaching of the Pastoral Epistles (so Conzelmann, who notes the linguistic peculiarities of these few verses with parallels in 1 Tim. 2:12; cf. Col. 3:18; Eph. 5:22) or inserted by a "corrupter" of the Pauline tradition determined to check a rising feminist movement in Asia Minor (Dennis R. MacDonald; see earlier, p. 76).

One of the strong points in favor of the latter suggestions is that the flow of the apostle's writing is more even if verses 34–35 (36) are left out. There is also some textual irregularity in that Western readings D G Old Latin place verses 34 and 35 after verse 40; and this is taken to mean they are a marginal gloss later copied into the text. The Western reading may also be an attempt to attain a smooth transition from verse 33a to verse 36 (so Zuntz).[15] The purpose of the insertion is either to moderate the Pauline charter of feminine equality (in Gal. 3:28; so MacDonald) or to reconcile 1 Corinthians 14 with chapter 11 (so Bittlinger),[16] or to bring 1 Corinthians 14 into line with 1 Timothy 2:12ff. (so Scroggs).[17]

Yet each of these expedients is less than satisfactory, and we should strive to excel in the gift of interpreting the text as it stands before we embrace these devices. Paul is not likely to have contradicted himself so quickly after writing 1 Corinthians 11:5–16, though MacGorman notes the paradoxical way Paul can give two seemingly exclusive sets of advice in this letter (1 Cor. 8:4–6 and

10:21). [18] MacGorman seeks to take refuge in our ignorance of all the local customs and conventions prevailing at Corinth, a view partly championed by Barrett and Koenig. Paul remains committed to social egalitarianism in the gospel (Gal. 3:28), and there is the undeniable evidence of the role he accorded to women colleagues (Phoebe, Prisca, the women of Philippi [Phil. 4:3], and the several women coworkers in Rom. 16). It is *prima facie* unlikely he should state categorically "let your women keep silent" in worship.

Therefore we should press the exegetical inquiry further. There are five options in handling the precise wording of the text.

(a) Women's voices were causing interruption in the services. The root problem, in this view, is that women were disturbing the proceedings at worship—especially when prophecies were being given—by asking questions that could more properly be put at home (F. F. Bruce; Sevenster, who imagines a heated discussion developing between husband and wife). [19] But it is difficult to see how Paul's stern injunction not only to keep silent but to be "in subjection" can be fitted into this context. And how does "the law" speak to this ban on women, cautioning them to remain silent? [20]

(b) Sometimes linked with the notion, derived from the synagogue, that men and women were segregated and physically separated in the Corinthian assembly, a similar view is that women were resorting to loud conversation among themselves. C. K. Barrett speaks of "feminine chatter"; the cause now is that women's strident voices were breaking the needed silence in worship by their frivolous chit-chat. What motivates Paul here is a concern for "peace and good order," and he comes down harshly on women, forbidding them to "speak" (*lalein*). But, as we have seen, this verb is otherwise used in the context of these chapters for glossolalic speech, not ordinary conversation.

(c) Based on the sense of "speak" (*lalein*) as "inspired speech," another interpretation attributes the root problem to women practicing glossolalia in the assembly. What Paul is rebuking is the way women were upsetting the good order of the worship by bursting out in a tongue and making utterances which, cast as questions, disturbed the proceedings when the gift should have been "under control." The merit of this view is that it enables us to take "be in subjection" as referring not to their husbands but to their own spirits, assuming that glossolalics could control their

utterances (14:28 says as much: "let them keep silent in the congregation"). It also seems to distinguish what is proper in the
setting of a home (where Paul locates the exercise of glossolalia for
personal reasons; 14:28) and what is "not permitted" (*ou epitrepetai,*
v. 34; cf. v. 35: "it is shameful for a woman to speak *at church*") in
the public assembly.

The residual difficulty with this otherwise attractive view is to
know the reason why Paul counsels women who "wish to learn" to
do so at home. The tongues-speaker is not usually regarded as a
person wanting to be taught.

(d) Margaret Thrall has set forth a solution, recently championed and developed by W. A. Grudem and J. B. Hurley,[21] that
it is women's interpretative action in respect of the prophets that is
under attack. Thrall writes:

> The only possible answer to the difficulty is that here Paul is referring
> not to a woman's exercise of the gift of prophecy, which he did not
> forbid, but to the practice of women joining in the congregational
> discussion of what a prophet or a teacher had said.[22]

The later treatments of this same idea refer to women who
sought to weigh what the prophets had said and so were "judging
the prophets." Aside from the inherent difficulty with the idea that
anyone in the congregation could judge (or was in fact judging) the
prophets as distinct from their oracles—a point made by
Dunn[23]—it seems strange that Paul would at one and the same
time grant to women the function of prophet and yet deny to them
the responsibility of evaluating what the prophets had said. If
women exercise a prophetic ministry (granted in 1 Cor. 11:5), we
would expect that they are to be included in the language of
1 Corinthians 14:29: "let the others judge."

Furthermore, can "speak" (*lalein*) mean "judge" in the sense of
diakrisis? When Paul talks of this gift in 1 Corinthians 12:10 he
does not breathe a word of restriction to imply such a charism is *not*
open to women. And what has "the law" to do with women not
judging the prophets? At least two Old Testament prophetesses,
Deborah and Huldah, exercised considerable authority.

(e) We revert to explanation (c) and offer a variant possibility.
This takes off from Robertson-Plummer's observation that the
Corinthian women were pushing to an extreme (which Paul re-
garded as illegitimate) their emancipated status. They had dis-

carded the veil (1 Cor. 11:5) and were putting in a bid for equality with their husbands not simply as fellow believers (a status Paul accepted in Gal. 3:28, though we should remark on its amazing novelty in grace, a "breakthrough" as Stendahl calls it)[24] but as *teachers of men in the congregation,*[25] a role that led them into erroneous views.

Their primal error is, then, a wrongful aspiration to be charismatic teachers, "speaking" in inspired language and laying claim to introduce fresh revelations that they were not willing to have assessed and corrected by the assembly and in accord with apostolic standards. Support for this view rests on the following grounds: (*i*) Its language, especially in verse 34, links it with 1 Timothy 2:8–15 where the issue is exactly the claim of upstart women teachers, possibly Gnostics. (*ii*) They are cautioned to restrain their desire to "usurp authority"; rather let them keep their prophetic spirits "under control," as "the principle" (*nomos*), that is, as Paul's earlier teaching prescribed. I take this allusion to be to no identifiable Old Testament reference but to Paul's own "ruling," "norm" (*nomos*), picked up in verse 37: "what I write to you is from the Lord." (*iii*) The role of a gnosticizing teacher does not warrant the women "speaking" in the assembly, even if they do have the gift of prophecy. Any interrogating (*eperōtan,* in the sense of "inquire after") of apostolic authority should be confined to the setting of the home, in accord with the Pauline household code (Col. 3:18; cf. Eph. 5:22; 1 Tim. 2:11–15). (*iv*) As a clinching argument, an appeal to 1 Corinthians 14:36 makes it clear, it would seem, that the matter of "the word of God" is precisely *the* central issue at stake. The Corinthians were claiming to have originated the divine message, with their women giving the lead. Paul forcefully denies this in his rhetorical questions, and proceeds to assert his apostolic authority (vv. 37, 38) over against a specious claim being registered by the Corinthian church as a whole. They imagined they were the sole repository and special conveyors of divine truth, and Paul's rebuke is to deny this claim at its source and to put his finger on the place where the claim was most articulate, namely, in the arrogation by certain women glossolalics of the office of "heretical" teachers and leaders.

Looking ahead (to ch. 15:12–20, 35–50, which will be examined in due course), we may suggest the specific cause of this phenomenon, that is, that women members of the Corinthian congregation were laying claim to a teaching at odds with the Pauline and apostolic proclamation. In summary, the root error was a denial of a future resurrection on the strength of what had supposedly occurred in baptism. Some Corinthians (15:12) were denying the resurrection because they claimed to be raised already. And this claim may well have carried with it—on the part of the women—a tacit denial of their married state on the ground that as "risen ones" they no longer owed any marital allegiance (see Luke 20:35, 36; 1 Tim. 2:11–15, which may or may not be linked with the aberration referred to in 1 Tim. 4:1–3, 7; 2 Tim. 2:18).[26] Rather, they regarded themselves as angelic beings, practicing glossolalia as the "tongues of angels" (13:1). Paul rebuts this position by recalling them to their marital obligations (14:35: "let them ask *their own* husbands at home") as part of his insistence that the Corinthians are still in this "mortal body."[27]

Translation

1–11   I make known to you, brothers, the good news which I proclaimed to you. You received it; you stand firm by it; through it you are being saved, *if you hold fast*[a] to the message which I proclaimed to you—unless *you believed*[b] in vain.

I handed on to you, then, as a top priority what *I* also *received*:[c]

that Christ died for our sins
    in accordance with the Scriptures;
that he was buried;
that he was raised on the third day
    in accordance with the Scriptures,
and that he appeared to Cephas;
then to the twelve.

After that he appeared to more than five hundred brothers at one time, most of whom live on to the present day, but some have fallen asleep (in death).

After that he appeared to James, then to all the apostles. Finally he appeared *to me*[d] as to *one abnormally born,*[e] as it were. I am the least of the apostles. I am not worthy to be called an apostle, because I persecuted the church of God. But what I am, I am by God's grace; and his grace in my case has not been ineffective, but I toiled more than all of them, yet not I, but the grace of God (working) with me. Whether then it was I or they (who labored), this is what we proclaim and this is how *you came to believe.*[f]

12–19   If Christ is proclaimed as raised from the dead, how is it that some among you say that *there is no resurrection of the dead?*[g] If there is no resurrection of the dead, (it follows that) neither has Christ been raised. And if Christ has not been raised, (it follows that) then our proclamation is empty, and your faith is empty as well. Also we are found to be false witnesses about God, when we testify *against God*[h] saying that he raised Christ. But he did not raise him if in fact the dead are not raised. For if the dead are not raised, even Christ has not been raised. And if Christ has not been raised, your faith is futile, you are yet in your sins. Then also those who fell asleep (in death) in Christ perished. If in this life *we are those who have set our hope in Christ only,*[i] we are the most to be pitied of all people.

Points to Ponder

a. The variant in D G ὀφείλετε κατέχειν, "you ought to hold it fast," makes the point clearer. See G. Zuntz, *The Text of the Epistles* (1953), 254ff.

b. Possibly an ingressive aorist, "you came to believe," going back to the Corinthians' conversion. See on v. 11.

c. Two technical verbs for receiving and handing on a tradition, corresponding to rabbinic Hebrew (*qibbēl, māśar*). What follows is a credal formulary or *paradosis* (tradition), prefaced by ὅτι recitative.

On the Semitic background see J. Jeremias, *The Eucharistic Words of Jesus* (ET 1966), 95ff., 101–105; and R. P. Martin, *New Testament Foundations* (1978), 2:251–52.

d. κἀμοί may give problems: it is crasis for καὶ ἐμοί.

e. One of several translations possible for ἔκτρωμα, lit. "miscarriage," "abortion."

f. See b.

g. Evidently a Corinthian watchword, at least among some of them.

h. κατά + genitive = "against."

i. A complex sentence, centering on two matters: the periphrastic tense (ἠλπικότες ἐσμέν, translated "we are the people who have hoped") and the position of μόνον. I take the adverb with the verb: we are those who have set our hope in Christ only (i.e., as the risen one, but not including the prospect of the believers' future resurrection). Paul (in my view) has the realized eschatologists at Corinth in mind. His periphrastic tense is then matched by "we are the people most to be pitied"— if this position is true.

CHAPTER SIX

THE RISEN LORD

THE ISSUES TO BE FACED

In 1 Corinthians 15:1–19 Paul moves, somewhat abruptly so it seems, to address a new theme: the resurrection of the dead in the light of Christ's own resurrection. The apparent swiftness of this turn in the apostle's thought has to be explained. One view is that he is dealing *seriatim* with the Corinthians' questions; so after handling matters of their public worship, he directs his attention to what was a further problem at Corinth, namely, that some were denying "the resurrection of the dead" (15:12). F. F. Bruce[1] writes: "Learning that some members of the Corinthian church were denying the doctrine of the resurrection as he had taught it to them, he deals with the subject in some detail," first by rehearsing the gospel message and showing how integral the resurrection is to that preaching. According to Bruce, this explains the reason for a lengthy recital of the apostolic kerygma of Christ's resurrection before he comes to verse 12, where the Corinthian problem is at length revealed.

Conzelmann, on the other hand, is so impressed by the introduction of a new theme "without transition" from chapter 14 that he states, "Chapter 15 is a self-contained treatise on the resurrection of the dead." And he notes that it is not until verse 12 that the application of the topic to the reader becomes clear.

The connection with chapter 14 is, however, probably more essential than these suggestions would have us believe. For one thing, the introductory formula "Now, brothers, I want to remind you" (*gnōrizō,* lit. "cause to know" in the sense of "draw attention to," as in 12:3) tells us that "Paul is reminding the Corinthians of what they ought never to have forgotten" (C. K. Barrett, comparing Gal. 1:11). The issue at stake is, by common consent, the apostolic proclamation that was being challenged at Corinth, specifically—if our previous argument has weight in regard to chapter 14 and the claims being made by gnosticizing women prophets—by those who were subverting Paul's authority as apostle (14:37–39). He replies to that charge with several clear statements, each designed to enforce that "authority" he claimed as God-given and to insist that the Corinthians "*ought* to hold fast" (the textual authorities D G read this in v. 2).[2] So Paul is driven to assert the content of his "gospel" and its accompanying and validating "apostleship" as authoritative and binding on the Corinthians in the face of their pretensions to private revelations.

We should therefore see how Paul's opening section (15:1–11) appears to be specifically slanted to repel three accusations leveled at him by those who needed the rebuke contained in 14:37 and 38 and quite possibly the charismatic Gnostics, male and female, who were insisting that the "word of God" was *their* exclusive property and privilege (14:36).

(a) Their most obvious counterargument to Paul was *that he was no true apostle*. While the language is not as forthright as that in 2 Corinthians 10:10, the allegation seems clear in the rare term, quite otherwise inexplicable in verse 8: "last of all he appeared to me also, as to *one abnormally born*" (*ektrōma*). The root meaning of the Greek term is a premature birth, an abortion, perhaps in the sense of "one hurried into the world before his time," as Barrett translates. In what way could this be said of Paul? Perhaps in contrast to the Jerusalem apostles (the "pillar" men of Gal. 2:1–10) who had known Jesus in his earthly ministry, Paul had been "born without the full term of gestation." So this is a direct denial of his equality with the "Twelve" whose witness to the resurrection Paul invokes (15:5).

But the word *ektrōma* is unnatural in expressing this idea. Going back to Harnack, others have submitted that the term is one of abuse and used by Paul's enemies, who hurled it at him to dismiss him as a monster, perhaps in regard to his lowly demeanor (as in 2 Cor. 10:10), but more likely as a "freak" unworthy of claiming rank alongside the true apostles. Yet a third possibility follows the suggestion made by J. Munck[3] and elaborated by Th. Boman,[4] which appeals to Ephesians 3:8: "to me, who am less than the least [*elachistoterō*] of all Christians." It is proposed that the Corinthians made play of Paul's name (*Paulos* = *paulus,* in Latin, "the little one") and dismissed him as a "dwarf." The advantage of this suggestion is that it links up with Paul's own continued thought in verse 9, where he turns this criticism to his own advantage: "Yes, I am indeed the least [*elachistos*] of the apostles," but an apostle for all that since I have seen the risen Lord and have the indispensable qualification of being commissioned by him to his service (Rom. 1:1: "an apostle by calling"; cf. Rom. 1:5).

(b) The next accusation seems to have implied that *Paul preached only an individualistic message,* namely, his own version of the kerygma. These Corinthians were disputing that this "Pauline" brand of the proclamation was the only viable expression of truth (as implied in Paul's retort in 14:36). So the apostle must be at pains to show how his "preached message" (15:1, "the good news which I preached to you," a cumbersome piece of tautology in the Greek) was indeed the true message since (*i*) it has been validated in the Corinthians' own saving experience (vv. 1, 2); (*ii*) it must be adhered to if they are to continue in the faith; (*iii*) Paul himself "received" it by tradition—so it is not self-originated—and he passed it on to them as a "top priority" (*en prōtois,* v. 3); and (*iv*) it is none other than the same gospel shared by the other preachers and leaders in the early churches (v. 11: "whether then it is I or they, this is what we proclaim, and thus you came to believe" [*episteusate,* in the ingressive sense of the verb]). In such a context Paul formulates and recites the content of the kerygma as the common possession of the apostolic "college" of which he claims to be a part.

(c) The issue under active discussion at Corinth *certainly had to do with Paul's proclamation of the resurrection.* Evidently some of his readers were disposed to doubt Paul's placing resurrection at the center of his message. From verse 12 it seems that what was in dispute was *not Christ's resurrection, but the resurrection of believers.* As Conzelmann puts it crisply:

> Paul is not seeking to prove that Christ is risen. He can take this belief for granted. What he intends to elaborate is rather the expression "from the dead."

Their error may then have taken several forms. We may quickly dismiss the idea that the Corinthians were "materialists" or believers in some philosophical notion of immortality of the soul (like the men of Athens; Acts 17:18, 32), yet at the same time rejecting the (later Hebraic) belief in resurrection (so Lietzmann, Moffatt). Nor is there much to be said for the idea that they believed that only those who survived to the parousia would be saved (Schweit-zer).[5] The most adequate view, first stated by Julius Schniewind[6] and widely adopted since then, is that such people, referred to in verse 12, were a part of the church who had embraced Gnostic ideas. They held that with the coming of the Spirit and their baptism to initiate them to a celestial life here and now they had entered on a new existence. Their "baptismal resurrection" (re-ferred to in 1 Cor. 4:8) had given them the fullness of God's life; there was no more to come. They denied the "eschatological proviso" that Paul's teaching set to mark the boundary between the "already" of being saved and the "not yet" of final redemption at the parousia and the resurrection of the dead in a new bodily existence (a theme handled in 15:35ff.). This teaching anticipates the later Gnostic idea contained in 2 Timothy 2:18: "Hymenaeus and Philetus who have wandered away from the truth. They say that the resurrection has already taken place, and they destroy the faith of some" (cf. Polycarp, *Phil.* 7; *Gospel of Philip; Epistle to Rheginos*).

William Baird[7] has raised an objection to this identification, asking if "the opponents had originally acknowledged Christ's resurrection, why does Paul spend the first eleven verses of chapter fifteen arguing for its reality?" The answer to this specific objection would seem to lie in the syllogistic nature of Paul's argument that leads to the conclusion in verse 16: "if the dead are not raised, even Christ has not been raised," a conclusion he knows they will deem unacceptable since it would contradict their assertion of being "raised with Christ" in baptism. So verse 12 is linked with verse 16 by a kind of inclusio (A–D) frame:

A Christ has been raised [all are agreed]
B Christians will *not* be raised [some allege this]
C If B is true, however, then
D A is untrue [and the Corinthian position is illogical]

We may add one further factor to this attempt to isolate and describe the pastoral situation that occasioned Paul's chapter, and it will answer additionally Baird's critique. Paul has cited a pre-formed credo (in vv. 3–5) that includes the statement "that Christ has been raised." In verse 12 he supplements the credal formula with the phrase "Christ is proclaimed as raised *from the dead*" (*ek nekrōn*), which he repeats in verse 20 with the further designation

"the firstfruits of those who have fallen asleep" in death. Conzelmann calls our attention to the fact that Paul does *not* say that
Christ is the firstfruit of those who *are to be raised,* as would be
natural to expect, but "of those *who have died.*" Conzelmann sees
this phrase (*ek nekrōn*) as warding off fanaticism by asserting that
only Christ has been raised; believers will have their resurrection
later, "in due course" (15:23). Paul is thus tacitly opposing the
claim to baptismal resurrection made by his opponents who may
have charged him with underplaying the present reality of "new
life now" by his insertion of the "eschatological reservation" of
what is only possible at the parousia and the onset of the end time.

The key term, then, seems to be "from the dead." The Corinthian enthusiasts were willing to grant a credence to the keryg-
matic-credal statement "Christ is raised" because they were
professing to be "risen with him" already. Paul anchors the kerygma in a resurrection *from the dead,* thereby asserting that death is a
precondition to new life (as in 15:36), and there is no resurrection
unless Christ really died (hence the creed is cited, including the
affirmation "he was buried" as a certificate of a true death), and
similarly Christians too may well have to die before the end comes
and they are raised (though at 15:51 he envisages some surviving to
the parousia, but even these need bodily transformation before
they can attain their resurrection; 15:50). We suggest, therefore,
that this is the nub of the debate between Paul and his Corinthian
opponents on the score of the resurrection. They were accusing
Paul of robbing them of their baptismal exultation of having
"come into the kingdom" here and now. Presumably this experience conferred a present immortality, and they may have expected
never to have to die. Paul's position lay diametrically opposed to
this on the grounds of the following: (*i*) the resurrection of the Lord
required his *prior death,* certified in his entombment; (*ii*) his resurrection is indeed the guarantee and ground-plan of believers, but
they too must reckon with having to die; (*iii*) yet believers who die
in the necessary interim between the present and the parousia are
not lost (v. 18); and (*iv*) as a final retort, "if in this life our hope is
only in Christ" (and his solitary resurrection)—and precludes a
resurrection of the Christian dead in "spiritual bodies" (15:44)—
"then we are the most pitiable of all people" (v. 19). Senft considers the other possible meanings of verse 19, conceding that the
view given above has ancient support.

PAUL'S APPEAL

If we are right in thus "reading between the lines" and observing the allegations brought against Paul which indeed occasioned this chapter, these are serious charges. Paul minces no words in making his reply clear and forthright. The question presents itself, How then does he respond? In a sentence, *he anchors the church's preaching—and so his own apostolic status—in the risen Lord*. By insisting that if Christ is not the living one who was raised and will at his parousia raise his people, Paul concludes, in logical fashion, that there is no meaning for the church's existence now and no hope for the future. This makes Christ's resurrection "the Archimedean point on which all else turns," W. Künneth's memorable phrase.[8] Paul will deal with these fateful consequences "if Christ be not raised . . ." in verses 12–19. But first we must set down the manner of the apostle's argumentation and, in particular, see how he proceeds logically to build his case in defense of his gospel and his apostolate. There are three lines of approach.

(a) *He begins by reciting the creed* (15:1–5). The churches of the New Testament period were already confessing companies of men and women as well as worship groups. By "confessing" we mean the possessing of a body of authoritative "doctrine" that was the given, acknowledged, and shared heritage of those who formed the early communities of faith in the world of the Roman empire. Only on the assumption of such a corpus of doctrine (however rudimentary and situation oriented it may have been initially) that was accepted as normative and binding on converts and adherents can we explain two attested phenomena of primitive Christianity. One is the consciousness of the church's being a distinct entity in the world over against both Jews and Gentiles (1 Cor. 10:32). Obviously this is more evident in the Pauline mission churches, which claimed a distinctiveness that later became undergirded by a theological conviction of the church as "one new person" replacing both Jewish and Gentile groups, and forming a "third race" (*tertium genus*) as in Ephesians 2:11–22.

The other factor is the church's missionary zeal, which from the beginning—at least from the time of the hellenists of Stephen's circle[9] (Acts 8:4; 11:19–21; 13:1–3)—exhibited a concern to proclaim the good news to all people. This message was offered not as a tentative suggestion to be entertained along with other attractive and viable possibilities but as God's saving truth, demanding a full and unreserved commitment (Gal. 1:8, 9; 1 Thess. 2:13; 2 Cor. 11:4f.). It is this explicit declaration of what the "gospel" is and how it held for Paul an unrivalled place as the expression of God's redeeming power (Rom. 1:16, 17) that gives us a background to 1 Corinthians 15:1 and 2:

> You received it [the gospel]. You stand firm in it; you are being saved by it [if you recall] with what form of words I proclaimed it to you. You ought to hold it firm [reading D G]—unless you came to believe to no avail.

The main tenets of a "creed"—or a piece of agreed teaching that Paul and his Corinthian readers shared in common—are now recited in verses 3–5. This is the most generally accepted demarcation of the quoted material in verses 3b–5, following K. Wegenast. [10] Introduced by a pair of semitechnical expressions ("I *handed on* to you . . . I also *received*," corresponding to the semitic verbs for the transmitting and receiving of a tradition from one generation of Jewish teachers to another), the next few verses contain a carefully constructed formulation:

> that Christ died for our sins in accord with the Scriptures;
> that he was buried;
> that he was raised on the third day in accord with the Scriptures;
> that he was seen by Cephas

This is clearly a crystallization of the same early church's teaching. (Whether it originated in Jerusalem or a hellenistic Christian center such as Antioch or Damascus is still unclear; the evidence for a semitic source is presented by Jeremias, for a Greek-speaking origin by Conzelmann, and for a mediating view of a Palestinian credo reformulated in a Jewish-hellenistic milieu and used in a baptismal confession by J. Kloppenborg.)[11] Certain telltale marks of the passage stamp it as a credal formulary: (*i*) the fourfold repeated "that" (*hoti*) introduces each line of the creed (vv. 3, 4, 5); (*ii*) the vocabulary is unusual, containing rare words ("sins" in the plural is not typical for Paul; similarly "he appeared") and expressions that Paul never uses elsewhere, such as "in accordance with the Scriptures"; his normal phrase is "as it is written" (twenty-nine times) or "Scripture [singular] says" (six times);[12] (*iii*) the parallelism of the lines; (*iv*) the dependence on Isaiah 53, which in other places betokens the presence of quoted material (e.g., Rom. 4:24f.); and (*v*) the emphatic preface of verse 3, which indicates that Paul is drawing on precomposed tradition and utilizing it as part of his appeal to accepted apostolic belief (v. 11).

Of more general interest and importance is what were the chief points of this early "confession of faith." It is not difficult to isolate the four "members" of the statement: (*i*) Christ's death has soteriological value since he died both "to deal with our sins" (*hyper tōn hamartiōn hēmōn*) and to fulfill the Old Testament prophecies (presumably Isa. 53 where the servant of God lays down his life as a sin-offering for many and "bears their sins" by being "handed over" for them; Isa. 53:12 LXX). (*ii*) Christ's real death, perhaps in the face of an incipient docetism and as part of Paul's argument that "death is a precondition of resurrection," is attested by the note of his burial. Whether this verb contributes anything to the question of Paul's knowledge of the empty tomb tradition is really beside the point. What Paul's recital of the creed, which presumably the Corinthians believed, implies is that the Lord's burial guarantees that his resurrection lay on the other side of his earthly existence. It is thus Paul's counterthrust to the Corinthian notion of a resurrection experienced *in this life* (a position denied in 15:36). (*iii*) The formula proceeds to state a vindicating resurrection ("he was raised," i.e., by God, as a "divine passive" demonstrating that "life out of death" is a miracle wrought by God [so Jeremias], as Paul will go on to argue in 15:38). The appeal to "the Scriptures" is not easy to understand, and we can only guess what Old Testament passages are in mind, whether general (as in Rom. 1:2–4) or particular (Isa. 53:11, 12; or, if the phrase is attached to "on the third day," then Hosea 6:2 LXX).[13] (*iv*) The personal appearances of the risen One to Peter, then to the Twelve (evidently a technical term for the Jerusalem apostles), then to over five hundred brethren, and then to James, the Lord's brother, and all the apostles, are designed to accomplish at least two objectives. First, they show the lines of continuity between the first witnesses so that their testimony is seen to form a unity (so W. Marxsen)[14]— a fact Paul needs as a basis for his later assertion in verse 11, "whether I or *they*." Second, they bring his list, after this impressive build-up, to a climax in the remark, "last of all [the immediate antecedent of this *pantōn* is "apostles"] he appeared even/also *to me*" (*kamoi* in an emphatic position). The resurrection epiphany is thus linked to Paul's apostleship.

So Paul has added to the preexisting credo, with reminders that the Lord appeared not only to Peter, as the precanonical gospel tradition rightly stated, but to others, and in that latter group Paul himself claims an honored place, even if his person is disdained (as an *ektrōma*, a misfit) and his name possibly suggested to his critics his insignificance (the "midget," *paulus,* as we observed).

In all this Paul is putting in his bid to be reckoned with the acknowledged leaders and witnesses to the resurrection. Tied in with that claim is his own commission to service, exactly as in 1 Corinthians 9:1 (cf. Rom. 1:1–4). It could be that he is registering some further claim to be numbered among those who fulfilled the requirement laid down in Acts 1:22, namely, "to be a witness of," or "witness to his resurrection"—a credential Luke evidently regarded as met in Paul's case (Acts 26:16).

(b) *He continues by reviewing his call* (15:6–11). Modern discussion of Paul's entry upon new life as an adherent of Jesus the Lord has tended to downplay the elements of disjunction between what he was before, a pious Pharisee and zealous observer of Judaic practices (Gal. 1:13, 14; Phil. 3:4–6), and what he subsequently became, a man in Christ (2 Cor. 12:1). This view sees the transition point as a bridge connecting his former life with his later career as a missionary preacher, and interprets Paul's own self-evaluation as a response to the Lord's call and commission, much as the Hebrew prophets (Isaiah, Jeremiah, Amos) heard and answered the divine summons. This reconstruction, eloquently stated by K. Stendahl,[15] is to be resisted on various grounds such as those I have listed elsewhere[16] and to which others, S. Kim in particular,[17] have recently called attention.

The issue in verses 6–9, however, *does* turn on Paul's appointment to the office and mission of apostle. The reason is again to be sought in his defensive posture vis-à-vis the Corinthians. He is continuing to ward off and neutralize the insinuation made at Corinth that he was no "true apostle" (2 Cor. 12:12 RSV). So he writes autobiographically of what he had become in spite of his dubious record as a persecutor of the church of God (v. 9); and he makes a twofold claim in all humility, saying two things about his ministry simultaneously. On the one hand, he concedes, "I am a

special case. I labored more than all the apostles and have creden-
tials (and scars) to prove it," as he said to the Galatians (6:17) and
will later recall to the Corinthian readers in his list of "trials"
(2 Cor. 11:23–29). His work as "pioneer missionary" (Rom.
15:20; 2 Cor. 10:12–16) is in view here. On the other hand, he
draws back from the use of the personal pronoun (comparable to
Gal. 2:20). The pronoun is inflected, as H. C. G. Moule points
out,[18] and D. M. Baillie has built this observation into his
christology on the basis of the Pauline aphorism, "*I . . . yet not
I . . . the grace of God . . . was with me*" (v. 10).[19] So Paul more
circumspectly phrases his life history: "Yet I owe it all to God's
grace at work in and through me; my service is not in competition
with others. And"—here he returns to his ruling theme in verse
11—"we all preach the same message and serve the same Lord."

So, in Paul's eyes, the verdict stands. He admits the intrinsic
unlikelihood (from a human point of view) of his ever becoming a
believer, let alone an apostle. But then he sees in divine grace (both
in drawing him to God and then empowering him, as in 2 Cor.
12:9, for service) the only explanation possible for such a transformation and such a record of exploits and endeavors. By God's grace
(*charis*) he became a Christian; and by the same grace (*charis,
suggesting charisma*) he has continued to fulfill his charge as "divine apostle," not least to those difficult, wayward, and suspicious
people at Corinth who were raising trouble for him and his message. His self-defense and *apologia pro vita sua,* he trusts, would not
fall on deaf ears or uncomprehending minds. To forestall that
possibility he has one further tack to pursue.

(c) *He rehearses his convictions* (15:12–19) in the light of the above
situation that was brought to the surface by the suggestion that
"resurrection" was a moot topic at Corinth. Again we recall that it
was not evidently Christ's victory over death that was at issue, but
the raising of his people at the end time (v. 12).

As we tried to show earlier, Paul's confrontation with the false
idea that "resurrection" meant only a baptismal exaltation to new
life in Christ with a consequent denial of a future resurrection led
him to stress Christ's resurrection as paradigmatic. He adds to the
credal statement "Christ was raised" (15:4) the significant phrase
"from the dead" to underscore his central affirmation. This assertion requires that "resurrection" can make sense only if it refers to
those who have died. In the case of Jesus Christ, he died and was

buried; then God raised him as a token of all future resurrections. In the matter of his people, they too must first face the reality of death before they can know the promise of resurrection. It will not do to deny the futurity of resurrection on the basis of a "collapsed" eschatology by which the future is brought into the present without remainder. This would be (*i*) to mistake the character of the Christian life now, as essentially existence "between the times" of the initial gift of God's grace and its consummation at the end of the age; and (*ii*) to cut the church off from the future God has intended, when all its enemies, including death, will be destroyed (15:24–28)—but not until then; and, on another level (*iii*) to confuse what for Paul is central, namely, the distinction between the "natural" body and the "spiritual" body (15:42–49). The Corinthian pneumatics, for all their claim to be "raised with Christ" now (picked up in Rom. 6:5–8; Col. 3:1–4) lived in earthly bodies, however much they sought to deny this fact, either by indulgence (1 Cor. 6:12–20) or by an encratite attitude toward normal marriage relations (1 Cor. 7:1–7, 36–40; and possibly 14:34–36, as we suggested earlier). They had forgotten that this earthly existence is *both* important—since the Lord "will raise us also" with Christ in the future (not as a past fact: only Christ has been raised so far, according to v. 12, as Güttgemanns suggests)[20] *and* only a foretaste of "the resurrection of the dead" (15:42). Paul must, therefore, go on to indicate some tragic consequences of surrendering this article of faith.

To do so, he offers a set of convictions in a negative fashion by postulating what would be lost if the twin affirmations that inextricably go together (v. 13) are denied. These are linked in the word *oude* at the center of the verse: "if [as you allege] there is no resurrection of the dead, *then* [or, *even*] Christ has *not* been raised." If the second proposition is allowed to stand, certain fateful results follow, which Paul proceeds to list: (*i*) Our proclamation (*kerygma*, the substance of the good news) has gone for nothing, since it is "empty" (*kenon*). "The resurrection is not an isolable fact," comments Conzelmann; indeed, it lies at the heart of Paul's preaching, as we can see from Romans 10:9, 10.

To evacuate Paul's message of the resurrection is therefore to take from it what he regarded as essential to salvation, and to deny to the cross its saving virtue, as the soteriological tag Paul quotes in Romans 4:25 recalls: "He was delivered over to death for our sins/And was raised to life for our justification." For Paul the cross lay at the center of Christian proclamation (1 Cor. 1:23–2:2), but only because he had the assurance that the crucified Jesus "lived again" by divine power (2 Cor. 13:4). Otherwise, the cross is emptied of its power as God's instrument of salvation. Only the living Lord can give salvation, won at the cross. As A. Schlatter put it: "No one can give to a dead man; no one can expect anything, or receive anything, from a dead man."[21]

(*ii*) Paul says virtually the same thing in the sentence, "and so is your faith" (v. 14; repeated in v. 17 with a change from "empty" to "futile" [*mataia*]). Denial of the resurrection renders Christian faith—*fides qua creditur,* the exercise of faith that leads to salvation—ineffectual, since that exercise fails to attain its goal. "Faith" that is not rooted in God's faithfulness in raising his Son from death to life—and so from defeat to victory and vindication—is disqualified as untrue to its name. "Faith" (*pistis*) goes back to the Hebrew *'emûnāh* whose root *'-m-n* is related to the idea of firmness, strength, and so confirmation—qualities that are impossible to associate with God if his purposes were defeated by death. So "faith" does not "work"—it is like a woman attempting to sew a fabric without a knot in her thread, to use Emil Brunner's homely illustration[22]—unless it has its object set in the God of the resurrection. In raising Christ he vindicated his character, validated his promises, and showed strength to overcome evil at its deadliest expression.

(*iii*) In verse 17 Paul relates this "triumph of grace" to the knowledge of forgiveness. "No resurrection, no gospel" is Moffatt's laconic way of focusing negatively on what for Paul would be a central element in the application of the good news to human experience: "You are still in your sins"; a plural noun for "sins" picks up the credal statement "Christ died for our sins" (15:3). The middle term is the assurance the resurrection of Jesus offers: that Christ's work as atoning sacrifice achieved the desired result and gained the pardon for his people that his death was intended to secure. The appeal is now directed to Christian experience, since Paul can elsewhere take it for granted that his readers have known what it is to be delivered by God from the dark dominion of evil and brought over into the kingdom of the Son whom he loves (Col. 1:13). The token of that transferral is the receiving of "redemption, the forgiveness of sins" (cf. Col. 3:13). On that shared fact of

experience Paul builds his case for the resurrection, since once
again without God's vindication of the crucified there is no certain-
ty that evil has been defeated and that its grip on human lives,
which were formerly at enmity with God (Col. 1:21), has been
broken and reconciliation achieved (Col. 1:22). Hence Paul inserts
into his paraenetic argument in Colossians the hymn of the cosmic
and victorious Christ who has brought about both universal harmony between heaven and earth and personal redemption whose
fruit is seen in a restored relationship between God and humankind, of which forgiveness is the sign and seal under the lordship of
the risen Christ. As E. Lohse writes:

> Whoever belongs to this Lord and has received the forgiveness of sins
> has thus also been wrested from the enslaving dominion of the cosmic
> powers and raised with Christ to new life. [23]

(*iv*) Further items of Christian conviction put in doubt by the
Corinthian denial relate to the church's hope for the future (15:18,
19). Verse 18 touches on what was evidently much debated at
Corinth, as some were wrestling with the paradox of bereavement
(cf. 1 Cor. 11:30) in the light of the teaching, which may be
known by inference, that Christians ought never to die. The prem-
ise for this latter idea is, we have seen, the appeal to a baptismal
resurrection by which believers were ushered here and now into the
divine kingdom (1 Cor. 4:8). We can see the effect of this teaching
in the (later) *Gnostic Treatise on Resurrection* from the Nag Hammadi
library (*Epistle to Rheginos* 44.46–45.68):

> The Savior swallowed death. . . . He raised Himself up (having
> "swallowed" the visible by means of the invisible), and gave us the
> way to our immortality. So then as the Apostle said of Him, we have
> suffered with Him, and arisen with Him and ascended into heaven
> with Him. . . . This is resurrection of the spirit [*pneumatikē anastasis*
> in the Greek version], which "swallows" resurrection of the soul along
> with resurrection of the flesh. [24]

The sad experience of loss by death would throw this teaching
into confusion; yet at the same time it would raise the tender issue
of what had happened to such deceased loved persons. Paul states
simply and without further comment the inevitable consequence
of dismissing the future resurrection by its being subsumed under
a present experience of "being raised with Christ." That is, if there

is no future hope, it follows that such as have "fallen asleep in Christ," those Christians who have died, have perished.

Nor is the prospect for surviving Christians any brighter (v. 19). The text may be understood in several ways, depending on the meaning of the composite tense of the verb "we are people who have hoped" (*ēlpikotes esmen*) and the positioning of the adverb "only" (*monon*). (a) "If *only for this life* we have hope in Christ, we are to be pitied more than all men" (NIV, italics added). This is perhaps the most straightforward way of rendering the Greek (see the argument of Conzelmann and Kümmel that "hope" is usually positive in Paul's thinking), and the sense here is that our hope if it is limited to this life is a poor thing (Bruce). Or we could take it, as Weiss does, to imply that we are only "hopers," and so self-deceived, if Christ is not risen.

(b) The attaching of "only" to "hope" is supported by others (e.g., Moulton-Turner),[25] who give to "hope" a negative quality. Our faith is only worthless "hope" that will never be fulfilled if it does not center on God's promises of resurrection. C. K. Barrett suggests that the adverb "only" applies to the entire clause since it comes at the end and the difficulty with the periphrastic tense is thereby lessened. He renders: "If in this life we have hoped in Christ—that and nothing more—then we are the most pitiable of all men."

(c) I submit that it is possible (and preferable, given the context and the thrust of Paul's rejoinder to the Corinthians) to retain "only" as close as possible to the "in Christ" phrase. So we translate: "If in this life our hope is only in Christ [or, in Christ alone] and *his* resurrection, but not in our future resurrection [exactly the point disputed, according to v. 12], then we are most to be pitied." The call to "pity" is that we have no hope for the future since a fancied "baptismal resurrection" terminates only in physical death common to all mortals, with no prospect beyond, and it deprives us of our "hope of resurrection to eternal life"; equally, this view is a logical deduction from verse 18, which has announced the dismal news that if there is no future raising of the dead, any "hope" we have in this life for deceased relatives and friends has gone.

On every score, Paul's convictions have to be extrapolated from this catalog of consequences, all of which hinge on the supposition "if Christ be not raised" with its corollary "if there is no future resurrection" for God's people. His own credibility is at stake; he is shown to be a "false witness" (v. 15) on all counts, not least that he has falsified the kerygma the Corinthians received and by which they are supposedly living. So Paul must now turn to a positive affirmation, to countermand all the hypothetical considerations he has introduced in this paragraph. His ringing assertion comes at verse 20: "But now, in fact [*nyni de*], Christ *has been raised from the dead*"—a full phrase, heavy with its perfect tense, to rebut all he has insinuated earlier.

Translation

20–28 *But in reality*[a] Christ has been raised *from the dead,*[b] the firstfruits of those who have fallen asleep (in death). For because death (came on the scene) through a man, the resurrection of the dead (came) also through a man. Just as all people die in Adam, so also all *those in Christ*[c] will be brought to life, but each one in his own order:

Christ the firstfruits,
after that at his coming those who are Christ's,
Then the end, when he hands over the kingdom to God the Father,
    when he has rendered ineffective every rule and every authority
    and power.

For he must *continue his reign*[d] until he has placed all his enemies under his feet. The final enemy to be rendered powerless is death; for *"he subjected all things under his feet."*[e]
When it (Scripture) says that all things have been subjected, clearly this does not include the one who subjected all things to him. But when all things are subjected to him, then also the Son himself will be subjected to the one who subjected all things to him. The result is that God will be all things to all (*or pervasively sovereign*).[f]

29–34 For (otherwise), what will they achieve who are baptized *for their dying bodies?*[g] If the (completely) dead are not raised, why then are they baptized for themselves as dead persons? And why do we face danger every hour? I assure you by my pride in you which I have in the Lord, I die daily. If *as a mortal man*[h] I fought with beasts at Ephesus, what advantage would it be to me, if the dead are not raised? *"Let us eat and drink, for tomorrow we die."*[i]
Do not be led astray:

"Bad company corrupts good habits."[j]

Come to your right mind and *do not go on sinning.*[k] For some (of you) are ignorant of God.[l] I speak to put you to shame![m]

Points to Ponder

a. νυνὶ δὲ: a logical turning point.

b. Paul turns to the creed (15:4: ἐγήγερται), but adds significantly ἐκ νεκρῶν. This enables him to go on to ἀπαρχὴ τῶν κεκοιμημένων, "the firstfruits of those who have died," not "of those who have been raised," since his argument requires that, as yet, there are none in that category.

c. I take οἱ τοῦ Χριστοῦ (v. 23) to settle the issue of where ἐν τῷ Χριστῷ belongs in this verse.

d. Present infinitive.

e. Psalm 8:6.

f. An attempt to render πάντα ἐν πᾶσιν.

g. A notable crux. I follow J. C. O'Neill, *The Expository Times* 91 (1980):310–11. See R. P. Martin, *The Worship of God* (1982), 188.

h. One meaning out of several of κατὰ ἄνθρωπον. Or is Paul simply speaking figuratively as well as hypothetically? (See discussion in *Philippians,* New Century Bible [1980], 48, 49 on an Ephesian imprisonment.)

i. Isaiah 22:13.

j. A citation from the comic poet Menander.

k. Note μὴ + present imperative to denote "stop doing" something; see W. S. LaSor, *Handbook of New Testament Greek,* vol. 2 (1973), section 31.3331.

l. I take τινες to refer back to 15:12.

m. On 15:20–28 there are more exegetical helps in R. P. Martin, *New Testament Foundations* (1978), 2:408–17.

CHAPTER SEVEN

THE KINGDOM NOW AND THEN

LIFE OUT OF DEATH

This subtitle has been chosen with some care. It is intended to focus the reader's attention on Paul's continuing debate with his Corinthian interlocutors. Their voice can be heard in 15:12 where they were saying that "there is no resurrection *from the dead*"; the key here lies in the final words. Their root error was to deny the future hope of believers, imagining that their "spiritual resurrection" in baptism (1 Cor. 4:8) was all there was. They apparently *did* believe in "resurrection" (presumably of Christ himself), but *not* "from the dead."

Paul's continuing response opens at verse 20, where he has chosen his wording with regard to the needs of his antagonists. He begins with a resounding affirmation, canceling out the "if's" in the previous verses. The hypothetical clauses, each commencing "if Christ has not been raised," are replaced by some clear statements that look back to the credal confidence of 15:4, "he was raised on the third day in accordance with the Scriptures." But we must mark how Paul has enriched this statement. By adding the phrase "from the dead" he has emphasized the prior death of the Lord and so the subsequent resurrection as a divine fiat that inaugurated a new age. That for him and his readers is given as a foundation statement on which all else rests, for as C. K. Barrett remarks, "There is no Christian faith without this affirmation."[1]

We should be clear as to the nature of the assertion. Looking on to 15:36 and 38 ("How foolish! [lit. you foolish person!] What you sow does not come to life unless it dies. . . . But God gives it [the tiny seed] a body as he has determined") we can see the precise issue at stake. Paul wants to clarify the meaning of "resurrection." It is both "life out of *death*," with death a needful presupposition (just as Christ died first, and *then* was raised from the dead), and "*life* out of death," where life is not simply an earthly existence but a new creation.

Evidently the Corinthians were disposed to cast doubt on both these Pauline deductions from the shared creed. They imagined that their resurrection had already taken place in the absence of physical death; they therefore thought of their celestial life, now begun, as an extension of their mundane existence, with any future resurrection dismissed as otiose.

Paul rebuts these wrong-headed notions by designating the Lord as "the firstfruits of those who have fallen asleep." Both parts of this description are polemically slanted. "Firstfruits" (*aparchē*) recalls the first sheaf reaped from the harvest field at the Israelite Festival of Weeks (Lev. 23:10–14) as a token of the full ingathering and the celebration of harvest home later in the agricultural year. The point is two-pronged: Christ—and Christ alone—has been raised up to this time, a reminder that is a tacit refutation of the Corinthians' claim to be "raised" already, albeit in a spiritual sense; and Christ is the firstfruits of those of his people who have already died, not who have been already raised (Conzelmann). This implies that death has come to them as a natural consequence, and they are still awaiting their resurrection at some future time.

It would seem that Paul felt it necessary to offer an apocalyptic passage (vv. 22–28) in defense of his understanding of the position on "life out of death." He must unpack what these essential terms mean, and say when it will be that death will give way to life. Hence he presents a piece of "salvation-history" in miniature with particular reference to these two questions: Why is death so rampant and pervasive in this present aeon, and how and when will death be defeated and brought under the control of an omnipotent, loving God? The "salvation-historical" (*heilsgeschichtliche*) interpreters of Paul, such as Cullmann, Kümmel, and Ladd,[2] have a preference for arranging the sequence of events in a timeline, and (without prejudice to the philosophical and theological underpinning of their schemas) we may follow suit. We proceed therefore to speak of the three phases of salvation-history according to the time frame of the three tenses of this section.

SALVATION-HISTORY IN THREE PHASES

(a) *Past*. "Christ has been raised" (v. 20) is Paul's point of departure, with the perfect tense of the verb not only harking back to the creed, but remarking on the continuing effects of an event that he would have "dated" in past time: "on the third day," that is, as an event in history.

For Paul history reaches back to the beginning of primal history. We see this in his contrast of the two Adams (vv. 21, 22), both representative figures and both the progenitors of a race intimately connected with them. From the first Adam, humankind derived only its separation from God and its inevitable penal consequence in death. From the last Adam who stands as the head of a new humanity, humankind received the promise of resurrection to life for those who are "in Christ."

Let us remember what Paul's purpose is in all this discussion. He intends to demonstrate that the resurrection of Jesus is bound up with—and gives promise of—the future resurrection of *all who belong to him* (not an elite group, nor a remainder who survive to the parousia while the others have been raised earlier in this life, as the Corinthians possibly were contending). If this line of argument is correct, it will help us to interpret aright the problematic word "all" in verses 22 and 28.

The upshot is that, within the categories of verse 22, "all-in-Adam die" embraces the entire race, whereas "all-in-Christ" is a limiting phrase, and Paul is concerned only to talk of resurrection in respect of those who belong to Christ (as in 1 Thess. 4:16). "All" in the second member of the parallelism "does not mean all men altogether, but all who are in Christ" (Conzelmann). And as a clinching argument, the future tense "shall be made alive" subverts the enthusiastic claim that they, even because they are in Christ now, have already received their resurrection. Paul does not deny them their standing "in Christ," but postpones their resurrection to an indefinite future (v. 23) when they will be called "those who are Christ's at his coming" (cf. 15:49, 52–54, which are all future tenses). The order in Paul's mind has to be fundamental: "the spiritual is not first, but the natural, and then [*epeita*] the spiritual" (v. 46), when it comes to the matter of the raising from the dead and the awarding of a resurrection "body." So the point is driven home: "each in his own order" (*tagma*, a military term for an army in formation, v. 23).

So Paul's thought moves to consider the "turn" of events that will form the future under active discussion at Corinth. Before we consider his teaching, we must pause to observe why it was necessary to stress the past and to consider the present as certifying the reign of Christ already begun. The first matter is fairly easily disposed of. His references to "death came [into the world] through one man" and "all-in-Adam die" seem clearly offered as evidential argument, drawn from Scripture, Jewish tradition, and human experience, to account for the prevalence of death, Christ's own death not excluded, throughout the race. With particular regard to his Corinthian disputants and partly to assist those who may have been genuinely puzzled over the incidence of death in the congregation (see 1 Cor. 11:30), Paul cites the sad and sorry case of Adam's fall and its baneful consequences (Rom. 5:12). Later he will return to this piece of traditional anthropology (15:47–49), all to emphasize humanity's kinship with "the man of dust" on whom was pronounced the sentence: "You are dust and to dust you shall return" (Gen. 3:19). No exemptions are possible to this general verdict on the inevitability of death, though two exceptions would need to be made in the case of Christ. First, he *chose* death as his destiny (Phil. 2:8), unlike the rest of humanity for whom death is a necessity (cf. Heb. 9:27); second, his short "interval" between death and resurrection rendered it possible for him not to be assigned to Adam's fate and return to dust, that is, to suffer corruption (cf. Acts 2:24–31).

(b) *Present.* The perfect tense of "Christ has been raised" (v. 20) offers the assurance that he continues to live. The argument goes a step further in verse 25 where it is the present infinitive that highlights the contemporary rule of Christ: "he must [continue to] reign" (*basileuein*). If we are correct in assuming that throughout this paragraph Paul's writing is argumentative with an eye kept all the time on the Corinthian scene, we can explain his allusion to the present reign of Christ in the following way.

So far Paul has been somberly negative in pointing to human-kind's involvement in Adam's loss and the sentence of death that has become universalized as humanity's condition. Yet the resurrection of Christ has spelled the dawn of a new chapter in world history, involving two aspects: (*i*) "Death" is often thought of in Jewish writings as a king or a kingdom that holds tyrannical control over its subjects.[3] Christ submitted himself to this control in his obedient death on the cross (Phil. 2:8; cf. Heb. 2:14, 15; 5:8) and entered death's dark domain. Later theology made much of this captivity during the *triduum mortis* (three days of death between Good Friday and Easter), based on hints in Acts 2:27, 31;

Romans 10:7; 1 Peter 3:18ff.; 4:6; Revelation 1:18.[4] But the clear teaching is that he emerged victorious and overthrew the powers of evil, whether on the cross (Col. 2:15), or more generally at his resurrection and/or ascension (Phil. 2:9–11; Eph. 1:20–22; 4:8–10; 1 Pet. 3:22; Rev. 3:21; 5:1–14). So the triumph of Christ, now exalted in the Father's presence and possessed of divine power, has broken the iron grip of evil on humanity, and opened the door of the kingdom to all believers. They have been "rescued from this present age" once under the power of the evil one (Gal. 1:4), and brought over from the dark dominion of Satan into the kingdom of the Son whom God loves (Col. 1:13), to share their inheritance with the angels (Col. 1:12).

(*ii*) Interestingly, the texts that proclaim Christ's lordship as a present fact are largely liturgical in character.[5] They picture the church at worship as it focuses that worship on the enthroned Lord, and they see God's total rule over all refractory forces *sub specie aeternitatis*, that is, as it will be at the end time when time merges into eternity and God's victory is complete. To be sure, the hymns and acclamations of the New Testament church at worship are expressions of faith since such hymns emerged out of times of trial and conflict. They represent no blinkered piety nor do they forget the present struggle with evil by seeking to flee from the world into a nirvana of unreal bliss in the divine presence. The songs of victory remain anchored in history, and never move far from the scene of redemption at the cross; but their vision is elongated to reach into the future to bring it near, and they can speak of Christ's future triumph as though it were present fact—*as indeed it is* to the church at worship caught up to the heavenly world.[6]

By contrast Paul, in 1 Corinthians 15:23–28, senses the danger of such triumphalism, and refuses to exult in Christ's present reign as though that was a reality all on its own. Notice, therefore, how he qualifies the declaration in verse 25. The rule of Christ has begun, he concedes . . . but it is not uncontested and it awaits that day in the future when "all his enemies" are set "under his feet," with the "last enemy" clearly identified as death (v. 26). At first sight it looks as if that subjection has already taken place (indeed, the hymnic passage in Eph. 1:21, 22 says as much). In verse 27, citing Psalm 8:6, Paul gives the submission as a past fact: "For God 'has put everything under his feet.'" But he then has to modify this quotation, which perhaps was being used as a proof-

text at Corinth by the realized eschatologists there who rejoiced in
the kingdom's fullness here and now, as they thought. So Paul
enters a double caveat. He remarks what is obvious with a moment's reflection, that God himself is not part of the present *regnum
Christi* since it is God who is the one who does the subjecting. Paul
needs to make room for a future *regnum Dei* as distinct from and
subsequent to a present *regnum Christi* (v. 24, which clearly sepa-
rates the two kingdoms). Christ's present rule is by its nature an
"in-between kingdom" (*Zwischenreich*, though this expressive
phrase is used also of a postparousia kingdom that lasts until the
end of the age) that is preparatory to the ultimate divine reality, of
which verse 28 speaks.

The other caveat comes in verse 28a, introduced by the words
"But when he has done this," or alternately if *ta panta* is the
impersonal subject of the verb, "But when all things are subject to
him [Christ]." Either way, Paul manifestly regards this subjecting
of "everything" to Christ as an event in the indeterminate future
that, logically, has not yet taken place.

What *is* a present fact is the inauguration of Christ's rule under
which the church presently lives; and if we may appeal to a parallel
passage in Paul (Col. 1:12–14), the token of that present lordship
is the holding back of the evil forces that no longer have power to
accuse the church and to separate it from God's love in Christ
(Rom. 8:31–39). Victory over malevolent powers is known in the
experience of the forgiveness of sins, and Paul has already linked
together forgiveness and Christ's work in death and resurrection
(1 Cor. 15:4, 17). The enemies of God's people are therefore
defeated *de jure* by Christ's resurrection triumph. Their final anni-
hilation and removal from the scene, however, awaits a *de facto*
judgment on them; and that, for the apostle, belongs to the "not
yet" needed to complement and complete the "already" secured
redemption won at Easter. The kingdom of Christ is now; the final
kingdom of God will be then.

(c) *Future.* So Paul's angle of vision widens to take in the future.
The pivotal "event" on which the future turns and by which
"history of salvation" (*Heilsgeschichte*) is shaped is called here "the
parousia," a Greek noun rendered by NIV "when he comes" (v.
23). And coupled with this central point in Paul's eschatological
discussion is his main preoccupation with the theme of death. The
latter evidently was the "sticking" point in the debate between the

Corinthian errorists (as he judged them) and Paul himself. They thought of death as a transition point from an earthly existence to a heavenly state, a *transitus* that had already occurred, at least for them, in baptism. All talk of a future resurrection was not so much wrong as unnecessary; and the "parousia" (lit. presence) of Christ was in the past and continuing into the present. Their entry into the kingdom was now.

Paul diametrically opposed this view. "Death," while already overcome in Christ's resurrection, still threatens and constitutes man's "*last* enemy" (*eschatos,* suggesting an enemy whose power will be with us until the end time, not just the last item in a series). History, radically altered by Christ's victory over the grave, will run its course until that end time. Then—and not until then—will the eschatological hope be made good, leading to the all-embracing sovereignty of God over all things (v. 28).

Paul's enumeration (in vv. 23–24) suggests the flow of events. "Each in his own turn" will be raised as the sign of death's being overmastered. (*i*) "Christ the firstfruits" takes us back to the associations of verse 20, and is a silent rebuke to those who might not have shared Paul's conviction that resurrection has not taken place for any but Christ alone. His resurrection is the promise of all future resurrections, that and no more. (*ii*) Then (*eita,* "next in sequence") "those who are Christ's" receive their share in the resurrection promise, but this will not be until Christ's parousia. Notice also the restrictive "those [people] who belong to Christ," which Paul has changed from the "all" in the preceding verses, just as he has altered the tense from a present to a future, as E. Schweizer remarks.[7] (*iii*) Then (*eita*; again, an adverb noting succession) the end (*telos*) comes, at which time Christ delivers over the (then present) kingdom to God the Father, having destroyed all dominion, authority, and power. These cosmic terms "represent the evil powers under whose control the world has come" (Barrett). The change in tense of the verbs *paradidoi* (present subjunctive) and *katargēsē* (aorist subjunctive) is not accidental. Christ "hands over" his kingdom when his final victory over his foes has been achieved and his enemies "destroyed." What Paul had envisioned as a process (1 Cor. 2:6, 8: such evil spirit-powers on the road to destruction) he now holds out as a realized event; in fact, Psalms 8:6 and 110:1 are introduced to demonstrate that Christ has these foes, including death itself, placed "under his feet." But that will be "at the end," which is the next and ultimate stage in the sequence (v. 28). "Then finally" is the way several interpreters (Barrett, K. Barth, F. C. Burkitt)[8] have understood the Greek *eita to telos*. The inference drawn on this view is that Paul's thinking has no room for an "interim kingdom" between the parousia and the end of all things, and Paul is simply passing on directly from the parousia to what follows immediately, namely, the resurrection of the (Christian) dead and the eternal kingdom. The resurrection is a "joyous" one, embracing only believers, and Paul seems here quite unconcerned about the fate of those not "in Christ."

The above reconstruction is only one way of construing a difficult—because compressed—passage. Some (such as Lietzmann and Weiss) wish to stress that after Christ's resurrection and then the raising of Christians at his parousia we should expect a third "group" (as a next *tagma* {v. 23]). That is the meaning, they insist, of "end" (*telos*), that is, the rest, whether the remainder of humankind in the general resurrection of the dead, or the Christians who have died in the interim between Easter and the parousia (as in 1 Thess. 4:16, 17) or between the parousia and the end (as in Rev. 20:5). This teaching is held as a support for a "millennial" kingdom in which Christ and his elect reign *after* his parousia yet *before* the handing over of the *regnum Christi* to God. And for Lietzmann the total conversion of humankind is placed in this interval, a view leaning to universalism. But it is extremely doubtful whether this scheme can be sustained. Héring has argued that *telos* cannot be paralleled in the sense of "the rest," and Paul is both here and elsewhere in his letters silent as to the resurrection of unbelievers; certainly he never suggests their conversion in any future millennial reign.

Telos may be taken, however, in the sense of purpose, as Conzelmann suggests. He notes the parallelism in verse 24: "*When* (*hotan*) he hands over . . . *after* (*hotan*) he has annihilated," and he relates these actions to what precedes. God has delegated his kingdom to Christ for a limited time (from Easter to his parousia) for the purpose (*telos*) of destroying the hostile powers. After this victory, Christ returns the kingdom to the Father; and Conzelmann finds here a rationale for the enthronement of Christ. God exalted him to reduce all opposition to divine rule to a vanishing point, so that "God may be all in all" (v. 28). This is an attractive way of making sense of Paul's somewhat obscure writing. It roughly corresponds with Héring's position, which gives to *telos* the force of a substantive: "then—it will be (*estai,* which is added) the end, when he returns the kingdom to God the father." This interpretation seems preferable inasmuch as it leaves open a *regnum Christi* between Easter and the parousia, but precludes a further "reign of Christ" after the parousia since at that time the penultimate rule of Christ merges into the perfected kingdom of God. This is what is meant by "the end"; not only "last in a series," but the finality and completion of all that God's purpose (*telos*) has been bent on achieving through the long haul of history.

The goal of history is attained by the Son's voluntary submission to the Father (v. 27; cf. 1 Cor. 3:23; 11:3) and the cessation of Christ's mediatorial reign. The Christ-hymn of Philippians 2:6–11 ends on the note of a universal acknowledgment, "Jesus Christ is Lord," but "to the glory of the Father"; so too in even clearer terms Paul spells out the implications of his Hebraic monotheism. God the Father and Christ perform, in salvation-history, different roles and operations *ad extra,* comments C. K. Barrett. As members of the godhead they share equal glory and honor; as differentiated persons within the unity of the godhead, they can be spoken of as superior (the Father is the "fount of deity" in the later phrase) and inferior (the Son is obedient and redeeming as God-in-revelation and God-in-redemption, to use Cullmann's terminology).[9]

But there is only one God, which is a fundamental Pauline axiom inherited from his Jewish past. Paul's concluding purpose in the soteriological drama is thus: "that God may be all in all" (*panta en pasin*).

Because Paul is not a speculative theologian and his vision of cosmic unity depends on how he sees God's outworking in salvation-history, which leads to a climax beyond history, we should not press these words unduly. To see in them a universalistic hope is proper, provided we recall that Paul has only Christians in his sights and views the problem of evil as a soteriological, not a metaphysical, knot to be unraveled. Perhaps his opponents at Corinth had leaped to a further unwarranted conclusion (as he would call it), that after the resurrection Christ merged with God by absorption into the divine unity. If so, Paul has refuted that already with his teaching on a *regnum Christi* lasting until the parousia. What he wished now to safeguard was the divine "monarchy" (or sole rule) lest the opposite deduction should be drawn that he held only a binitarian (or dualistic) picture of the godhead in which Christ was a second or rival deity. So he ends with announcing the goal of *Heilsgeschichte,* namely, that God's kingdom will then be finally established and God will rule "in all the universe and completely" (Héring). It is "the total and visible presence of the kingdom of God," he says, in its fullness.

TRUTH RELATED TO LIFE

Having defended his understanding of resurrection as a sure hope for the future since it is based on Christ's role as mediator in salvation-history, Paul goes on to show how this rich seam of truth impinges on life. His discussion of practical implications and influences is still dictated by polemical and pastoral considerations. In his view, to cast doubt on facts is to cut oneself off from factors meant to influence how a person lives. Conversely, serious denials of the resurrection, both Christ's and the church's, have a negative impact on personal and corporate behavior. He will touch upon three of the areas where the Corinthians had mistakenly and tragically started to act out their erroneous theological beliefs; and at the heart of this paragraph (15:29–34) stands once more the controverted issue of whether Paul's apostleship is genuine or not. We will survey these four matters, though the attempt to pinpoint the precise meaning of each of them is hindered by a lack of detailed knowledge on our part.

(a) If there is no resurrection hope, a dubiety expressed by his introductory *epei* ("since otherwise," as in 1 Cor. 5:10; 7:14), "what are those people who are baptized on behalf of the dead to do? If the dead are not raised at all [*holōs*], why to be sure [*ti kai*] are they baptized on their behalf?" (v. 29). At the center of these enigmatic questions lies the phrase "What will they do?" which, as Barrett points out, may yield two meanings: (*i*) What will they achieve for themselves or for others by getting baptized? and (*ii*) What will they do next, when they discover that their actions have been in vain, since there is no resurrection? The two ideas merge, but they leave us with an outstanding difficulty of knowing what kind of baptism Paul has in mind as he alludes to a Corinthian practice. This has led to a bewildering variety of interpretations.

According to K. C. Thompson,[10] up to 200 different explanations have been offered.

Clearly Paul knew the custom, but he cites the procedure of "baptizing for the dead" without necessarily agreeing with it or conceding that it is part of apostolic practice. In fact, he has already shown himself to be somewhat reserved about his practice of baptism (1 Cor. 1:13–17) in a church where the rite was subject to misunderstanding and distortion (1 Cor. 10:1–13). His train of thought is pointedly *ad hominem,* that is, he is utilizing what he knows of this Corinthian practice simply to argue that the custom they cherish has no value *on their terms,* if the dead are not raised.

There are three main views in the field of interpretation. The first, adopted since the early centuries when church fathers knew this kind of baptism to be a heretical practice of the Marcionites, is that the Corinthians were practicing *a vicarious baptism.* Some members (the Greek *hoi baptizomenoi* speaks of a class of Christians, not all the Corinthians who presumably were all baptized; 1 Cor. 12:13) of the church were receiving baptism in place of friends or relatives who had died (say, as victims of epidemic or by accident, as Rissi supposes)[11] before they could pass from the status of interested inquirers to that of full members of the church. The baptism was thus a proxy baptism. Two scholars (Maria Raeder and J. Jeremias)[12] turn this view around by wanting to read the preposition *hyper* as "for the sake of," that is, in a telic or final sense. In other words, "the dead" are believers and the pagan Corinthians were undergoing a vicarious baptism on their behalf in order to ensure a reunion with their deceased relatives after death. On both counts, vicarious baptism requires us to think of the Corinthians' faith in baptism as magical at worse or mechanical at best! Certainly it is a sacramental theory that requires the rite to act independently of personal faith or response, and one wonders if Paul would have used such a questionable practice, however much it may have been current coin among his readers (see 1 Cor. 10:1–13), if his understanding was so totally out of harmony with this *ex opere operato* view. M. Rissi[13] has endeavored to overcome this objection by maintaining, in defense of a vicarious baptismal practice, that the dead were Christians who had expressed their faith but who had been prevented by the onset of premature death from being baptized. In this view baptism functions—as a person is baptized—as a sign rather than as an effective means of union with or sharing in Christ, and it is the ceremony on his principal's behalf. But this still undercuts the nature of apostolic baptism (as distinct from the Corinthians' thought about baptism and its magical effects; cf. 1 Cor. 1:13–17; 10:1–12) as essentially personal and confessional.

Second, F. Godet[14] offers an interpretation that pays respect to the future tense, "what shall they do?" (i.e., what is to become of them?) and links verse 29 with its neighboring verses (30–32), where Paul raises the possibility of his dying for the faith. It interprets *hyper* to mean "with a view to," and suggests that what Paul is talking about is *martyrdom pictured as baptism.* The thought is that of Mark 10:38ff. and Luke 12:50, where Jesus speaks of death for others under the figure of being drowned in waters of suffering and woe. It is undeniable that a Christian's death for Christ's sake in the arena or at the hands of the Roman magistrates and soldiers was taken in later history to be the equivalent of his baptism, if he had not been able to enter the church's fellowship by the regular procedure of initiation. This is the so-called "baptism in blood." The preposition in verse 29, then, must be taken in the sense "to be baptized *with a view* to death," and the point of Paul's question is to raise the absurdity of a martyr's willingness to be baptized (i.e., to die) to join the ranks of the dead if there is no promise of resurrection. It is doubtful, however, if *that* is the point; furthermore, the preposition *hyper* has a more usual meaning of "on behalf of," which tells against this theory.

As a third option we call attention to the recent contribution of J. C. O'Neill, although we will seek to amplify his original suggestion.[15] We may build on two assumptions: (*i*) The verb "to do" (*poiein*) in its future tense carries the sense of "accomplish, achieve" (German *ausrichten*); and (*ii*) The phrase "on behalf of the dead" (*hyper tōn nekrōn*) does not refer to a third party but is in apposition to the subject "those who get themselves baptized." The whole phrase means "why do those baptized reckon themselves as dead?" Another component factor to be built into the translation is the Corinthian situation itself, which, as we noted, centered on a virtual denial of death on the supposition that Christians glide from this earthly existence to a heavenly state at baptism. Paul is therefore challenging this view once more by calling in question what the Corinthians were intending to do at baptism. The question in verse 29 is a *rhetorical rebuke aimed at showing how inconsistent is the Corinthian practice of baptism.* O'Neill paraphrases verse 29 as follows:

> Otherwise, what do those hope to achieve who are baptized for their dying bodies? If the completely dead (*holōs* qualifying *nekroi*) are not raised, why then are they baptized for themselves as corpses?

This interpretation may be further supported by the train of Paul's argument throughout the entire chapter, and it rescues verse 29 from being an isolated text, more or less without context, which speaks only of an erratic Corinthian practice. In this view the verse fits neatly into the pattern of debate between Paul and his readers (in vv. 12, 36). The issue is not resurrection *per se* but "death as a presupposition of resurrection," which the free-thinking, gnosticizing Corinthians were denying. They doubtless expected that they would never have to die—since they had "died" already in baptism, and were raised in and with Christ. Paul now indicates the fallacy of this position: their bodies baptized in water as "dying" (in the sense of 2 Cor. 4:10–12) will eventually become "corpses." What point is there in baptism unless it holds within its meaning for the convert the pledge of the "resurrection *of the dead,*" to be granted at the end time when "spiritual bodies" will replace decayed corpses (15:42–49)? Only in this view does the future tense "what shall they achieve. . . ?" gain its distinctive, eschatological value, since Paul deliberately chooses it specifically to direct his readers to what they were denying, namely, a *future* resurrection.

(b) If there is no resurrection, the apostolic hazards that exposed Paul to mortal peril continually (lit. "every hour," v. 30) are no better than foolhardy acts—a charge his enemies at Corinth would later bring against him (2 Cor. 6:3–10; 11:21–33). So Paul reverts to a central issue in this whole discussion: his authentic claims as an apostolic man. The argument here turns on whether he would have endangered his life and so "boasted" (a key term in the Corinthian correspondence) of his record as sincerely interested in the readers' welfare, if at the end of the day he would have nothing to show for it (as in Phil. 2:16: "in order that I may boast on the day of Christ that I did not run or labor for nothing").

His entire life of missionary and pastoral service was a facing of risks for Christ's sake and the well-being of the churches. "I die every day" (v. 31) must be taken figuratively, in the sense of "I face the reality of death every day." This manner of speaking puts us on our guard against taking the "fighting with wild beasts" at Ephesus too literally.[16] If it were an actual encounter in the arena when Paul was condemned *ad bestias,* he must have been rescued, like Daniel, by a marvelous divine intervention. After all, he did live to tell the tale! The phrase *kata anthrōpon* may mean "as a man," but that is tautologous, since how else could Paul have been exposed to death? An alternative meaning is "after the manner of men [who have no hope of resurrection]"; then Paul is pointing to the hopeless state he would have been in if he had no prospect of resurrection to cheer him in his trials (so Lietzmann, Schmiedel).[17] A third option is that taken by RSV, "humanly speaking," suggesting that he is speaking in metaphorical language and (perhaps) using a proverbial expression for deadly—but human—opposition (cf. 1 Cor. 16:8f.: many enemies at Ephesus; Ignatius, *Rom.* 5:1, uses the verb *thēriomachein,* to fight with beasts, of the soldiers who guarded him on his way from Antioch to Rome where, to be sure, he did face the beasts in the amphitheater). There is also the question of whether Paul as a Roman citizen would ever have faced the danger of capital punishment in this way. If he were allowed to plead his citizenship rights, the law protected him from such a fate; but G. S. Duncan's interesting monograph *St. Paul's Ephesian Ministry*[18] has pointed to a period covered by Acts chapters 19 and 20, when there was social anarchy in the Asian province following the assassination of the proconsul Junius Silanus in A.D. 54; and it may be argued that Paul's protestation of Roman privilege fell on deaf ears. But we face the argument from silence: if he was condemned to the beasts, why did he not explicitly refer to an amazing and providential deliverance (perhaps he does in 2 Cor. 1:8–10, however)?

Two remaining possibilities that need to be mentioned are really the only two viable options for interpreting verses 30–32. Is Paul referring to an event that seemed likely to happen but never did (so Weiss, Héring)? This implies that the conditional clause (if . . .) is unreal. But decisively against this is the preceding "Why do they get baptized?" and the parallel "Why do we stand in danger?" both of which postulate real situations, not imaginary cases brought in for argument's sake. We are driven then to sup-

pose a real, life-threatening danger that Paul faced at Ephesus that
cannot thereby be the situation of Acts 19:23–41. The occasion
left Paul no choice but to contemplate the end of his life (it may be
that Phil. 1:20–24; 2:17 refer to this extremity; 2 Cor. 1:8ff.
almost certainly does). It was, he says, like a man doomed to the
arena with no prospect of escape and no hope—except that for
Paul, "the God who raises the dead" (2 Cor. 1:9) came to his
rescue. But—and this is the point of Paul's appeal—even before
the deliverance came he had the assurance of "life out of death"
such as sustained the Maccabean martyrs (see Dan. 3:16, 17;
2 Macc. 7:14; cf. Heb. 11:35), and God brought him through.
Yet had he succumbed in the trial, his missionary labors would
have been crowned with a martyr's joy only because the resurrection is what made it worthwhile ("what benefit is it to me?" V. 32
is not opportunistic nor a kind of prudential reasoning of self-
interest. It is "gain" for the gospel of which Paul is a servant that is
in view, as in Phil. 1:12, 23, as K. Barth rightly notes on those
passages). [19]

(c) "If there is no resurrection"; Paul draws out a corollary as
background to verse 32b: so there is no final judgment. Christians
may as well adopt and live by the maxim "Let us eat and drink, for
tomorrow we die."

This couplet is taken from Isaiah 22:13, a saying in the tradition of Jewish wisdom teaching. Wisdom of Solomon 2:6ff. is a
partial parallel. But the more immediate setting is the pagan
philosophy of "live for today," typical of Epicurean skepticism in
Paul's own time (cf. Eccl. 2:24; 9:7–10, cited by Bruce). The
underlying idea is that this life is all there is and after death there is
only uncertainty. The conclusion stands: therefore, eat, drink, and
enjoy life to the fullest. For Paul this line of reasoning is contrary to
all his religious beliefs and practices, as both a Jew and a Christian
believer. God will bring every human activity into judgment, and
logically this necessitates that men and women are accountable for
their actions in this life because they will be called to a day of
reckoning in the next. This is precisely the thrust of the speech at
Athens (Acts 17:31: God "has set a day when he will judge the
world with justice by the man he has appointed. He has given
proof of this to all men by raising him [Jesus] from the dead"); but
the same serious attitude toward life in the face of a future judg-

ment is found also in Romans 2:16; 14:10–12; 2 Corinthians 5:10. And implied throughout this discussion is that only the resurrection ensures that Christ is Lord of the dead as well as the living (Rom. 10:9).

(d) A final warning rounds off this paragraph (vv. 33, 34). Quoting from Menander's comic play *Thais,* with an introduction "Do not be led astray" (in 1 Cor. 6:9 the same phrase sets the scene as a warning against immoral pursuits in the name of Christian "liberty"), Paul has his eye on some libertine practices that were related to his readers: "Bad company corrupts good character." Conzelmann asks whether this is a general warning against a tendency to live by the world's standards (Rom. 12:2), or a specific warning directed at those at Corinth who denied the resurrection. The application given in verse 34, "really come to your right senses" (*eknēpsate,* lit. "sober up," looking back to "let us drink" in v. 32 but possibly also to 1 Cor. 11:21, which describes drunkenness at the agape meal) and "quit sinning" (a present imperative meaning to stop what they were doing), points almost certainly to the latter interpretation. The Corinthian enthusiasts were "intoxicated" with their spiritual exuberance, and Paul answers them with the eschatological watchword to pay heed to the call to "keep sober" (1 Thess. 5:6–8). This implies that their baptismal theology had bred moral laxity and a lapse into antinomian ways that made them heedless of the strenuousness and vigilance required in the Christian life. Their orgy at the fellowship meal was one symptom of a bad theology that undercut ethical endeavor.

At fault also was their disregard of others, evidently outsiders—but the "some" (*tines*) could equally well refer back to the "some" of verse 12—who "have no knowledge of God" (here a play on the Corinthians' pride in *gnōsis,* 1 Cor. 1:5; 8:1; 13:2, 8).[20] It is shameful, Paul retorts, that some of the Corinthian elite as "people of the Spirit" have acted in this way without regard to the effect of their conduct on others. Worse still, they seek to justify their lax behavior on the ground that they are already risen with the heavenly Lord and they "know" the esoteric mysteries that have been imparted at baptism. For Paul baptism plays a quite different role. It ushers the believer into a new relationship with Christ whereby the "old nature" is put to death, and the call is renewed every moment: "count yourselves dead to sin but alive to God in Christ Jesus." The turning point of baptism is not enlightenment, ecstasy, false security (1 Cor. 10:1–13: orgies and immorality go together here, along with a blind trust in sacramental efficacy), and the claim to enter a heavenly world now, but rather:

> We were . . . buried with him through baptism into death . . . and united with him in his death . . . that we may live a new life . . . and we will certainly also be united with him in his resurrection. . . . Do not let sin reign in your mortal bodies. (Rom. 6:4–14)

Translation

35—41   But someone will say, "How are the dead (to be) raised? With what kind of body do they come?" Foolish person, what you sow is not brought to life *unless it (first) dies*.[a] What you sow is not the body that will be, but a bare grain, it may be of wheat or one of the other grains. But God gives it a body as he willed, and to each of the seeds its own body.

All *flesh*[b] is not the same flesh. There is one flesh of men, another of animals, another of birds, another of fish. There are celestial bodies, there are earthly bodies; but there is one glory of the celestial, another of the earthly. There is one glory of the sun, another of the moon, another of the stars. Indeed one star differs from another in splendor.

42—49   The resurrection of the dead is like that. (*The body*[c]) is sown in a perishable state; it is raised in an imperishable state. It is sown in disgrace, it is raised in glory. It is sown in weakness, it is raised in power. It is sown a natural body, it is raised a spiritual body.

If there is a natural body, there is also a spiritual body. Thus also it stands written:

> The first man Adam became a living person,
> the last Adam a life-imparting spirit.[d]

Yet the spiritual is not first, but the natural, and then the spiritual. The first man was out of the earth, a man of dust; the second man is out of heaven. The people of dust are like the man of dust, the people of heaven are like the heavenly man. Just as we have borne the form of the man of dust, we shall bear also the form of the heavenly man.

50—58   I declare this fact, brothers, namely, *flesh and blood*[e] cannot possess the kingdom of God, nor does what is perishable possess what is imperishable. Listen, I tell you a secret: we shall not all sleep (in death), but we shall all be changed, in an instant, in the blink of an eye, at the final trumpet-call.

> For the trumpet will sound, and the dead will be raised
>   imperishable,
> and we shall be changed.

For this which is perishable must clothe itself with imperishability, this which is mortal clothe itself with immortality. When this which is perishable has clothed itself with imperishability, and this which is mortal has clothed itself with immortality, then the word which is written will come (to fulfillment):

> Death has been swallowed up in victory.
> Death, where is your sting?
> Death, where is your victory?[f]

The sting of death is sin, the power of sin is the law. But thanks to God who gives us the victory through our Lord Jesus Christ.

Therefore, my dear brothers, be firm, unmoved, always *excelling*[g] in the work of the Lord, in the assurance that in the Lord your labor is not wasted.

Points to Ponder

a. A key phrase: see H. Riesenfeld, *The Gospel Tradition* (ET 1970), 171–86.

b. "Flesh" (σάρξ) here is the OT term: the stuff of which corporeal existence is made. There is another usage of Paul's term that makes it a designation of a person's sinful nature.

σῶμα (body), on the other hand, is Paul's basic description of human existence both in sin and in grace (v. 44).

c. Implied subject is σῶμα.

d. See J. D. G. Dunn, "1 Corinthians 15:45—Last Adam, Life-giving Spirit" in B. Lindars and S. S. Smalley, eds., *Christ and Spirit* (1973), 127–41.

e. σάρξ καὶ αἷμα: "flesh and blood," a term meaning frail human nature, and possibly a polemic against the Jewish and Gnostic idea of a resurrection of the physical/fleshly body (see *Gospel of Philip* 2.3, *The Nag Hammadi Library*, ed. J. M. Robinson; codex pages 56–57 on pp. 134f.).

f. On the OT as cited here, see E. E. Ellis, *Paul's Use of the Old Testament* (1957), 15.

g. περισσεύω: "excel, gain"—a Pauline keyword in his Corinthian correspondence. (1 Cor. 8:8; 14:12; cf. negative in 1:7 μὴ ὑστερεῖσθαι ἐν μηδενὶ χαρίσματι: "you are lacking no spiritual gift.")

CHAPTER EIGHT

THE RESURRECTION HOPE

INTRODUCTION

In a sense the discussion up to this point has been preliminary, although most needful. In brief, some believers at Corinth denied the resurrection *hope*, viewing the resurrection as a present reality, begun in baptism and the onset of spiritual life for those who were "raised with Christ" at that time in their experience; against these people Paul has entered several counterpositions required by the apostolic gospel. He has asserted (*i*) the pivotal event of the Lord's resurrection, which indeed included his people, but not to the exclusion of their future resurrection *from the dead*. Only Christ as "firstfruits" has been raised in that sense, though the token resurrection on Easter is a promise of a future hope held out to all who belong to him (15:23). The rule is, "each one [will be raised] in his own turn" (v. 23), an expression that Paul reverts to when he comes to develop an analogy of harvest (15:38). As we have suggested, he was possibly led to that illustration from the agrarian setting of the Jewish Feast of Weeks in which the "firstfruits" were presented as part of an orderly sequence that climaxed in the full harvest later in the agricultural calendar.

(*ii*) Paul has also shown the baneful consequences on Christian life, morality, and service of this false eschatology that denies a future hope. It cuts the nerve of ethical endeavor and leads believers to a wrong picture of Christian existence. The church is indeed called to be the community of the risen One, the fellowship of those raised to new life in Christ (Rom. 6:4; Col. 3:1). But Paul is careful not to say too much or to make too extravagant claims for this initial response to God's call. After all, God's work in the church has begun, to be sure; but its fulfillment awaits the future (Phil. 1:6); and only then—at the parousia and beyond, to be precise—will God bring his salvific purposes to their completeness. Christians, in the meanwhile, live in the "in-between" period, set between Easter and Christ's ultimate triumph, and they are subject to all the risks and trials inherent in their being "in the body": temptation, struggle with sinful tendencies, and their mortal destiny as men and women doomed to die since they exist simultaneously "in-Adam" as well as "in-Christ."

It seems that Paul's Corinthian readers—or some of them, at least—were entertaining contrary notions in regard to exactly these matters. They claimed, as Greek-thinking individuals, that once their spirits were "saved," their bodies were irrelevant, and no evil could touch them (Paul answers this in 1 Cor. 5:1–13; 6:12–20; 10:6–13). They also imagined that their entry into a kingdom already present (1 Cor. 4:8) gave them a passport to a heavenly type of existence where such items as unusual marriage customs (1 Cor. 7:36–40 refers to a kind of platonic union of minds, but implies a celibate relationship between the sexes, not unlike what they thought the angelic existence to be) and a privatized worship involving "tongues of angels" (1 Cor. 13:1) prevailed. Most characteristically, they seemed to have thought that they would never die but were already enjoying—in Gnostic terms—life in a hidden body. Such a body lay beyond "death" and simply continued to exist as a "spiritual body," a term (in v. 44b) that, as W. Schmithals and E. Schweizer remark,[1] meant *for them* a body composed of *pneuma,* "spirit"—man's original possession. To this "body" they already laid claim as "persons of the Spirit" (14:37, *pneumatikoi*).

So once again it is this reconstructed background that we must keep in mind as we move into 15:35–58, where Paul addresses, in a self-defensive, apologetic mood, the issues being raised at Corinth. In a sentence, he grants that while there is "victory in Christ" (his eloquent climactic statement, repeated three times in 15:54–57), its fullness will come only in the resurrection that lies beyond physical death, at the parousia of Christ, and as part of God's eternal plan to bring in a new age of immortality. These three terms (resurrection, parousia, immortality) modify the celebration of God's triumph. The Corinthians were acting as though the triumph were a reality now in this present age. Paul has to insert the "eschatological proviso" (*eschatologische Vorbehalt*) that in effect says, Not yet—but the end will assuredly come in God's own good time.

Evidently his disputants, listening to Paul's rebuttal of their position, raised some objections. We hear their voice in 15:35 as they tried to mock Paul's insistence on resurrection as a new bodily existence (so Schniewind, Brandenburger).[2] They offered two questions: How are the dead—no better than corpses—raised? With what kind of body do they come? Both questions depend on what they take to be Paul's teaching construed in a materialistic fashion and understood as if resurrection-life were simply a prolongation of earthly conditions. Obviously, they needed some clarification. Paul seeks to give it, possibly (as J. Jeremias suggests)[3] by reversing the order of these two questions. They are pressing him to say what he meant by the *nature* of the new corporeality; he answers this in verses 36–49. Their other question spotlights the *manner* in which he envisaged the resurrection process to take place; he responds in verses 50–57. Perhaps, however, the Pauline discussion is not so neatly tabulated as this.[4] We suggest alternatively that his reply falls into three areas:

1. In answering the question inspired by the denial of resurrection, which for Paul required a prior death, he offers a rationale based on the principle "life out of death" (vv. 35–41).

2. The next section (vv. 42–49) is devoted to establishing a sequence, again the subject of the Corinthians' questioning, which sets the pattern of our future body as based on that of the "heavenly man," Christ in his preexistent being. The time-frame is (a) Christ in his glorious body in eternity; (b) our earthly body now; (c) our future bodily existence, which is modeled on (a)—but in that order, reverting to 15:23.

3. Pressed to say what the new "body of glory" will be, Paul adds a final section (vv. 50–57) to dispel some wrong-headed ideas and then to describe, in apocalyptic terms, the coming of a new aeon that will be marked by death's defeat and God's victory. Verse 58 is a practical conclusion and exhortation.

THE RATIONALE OF RESURRECTION

"How are the dead raised?"[5] is a query that would spring naturally to the lips of any who had followed closely Paul's train of reasoning. The sharp point is put on the issue if it reflects a skepticism that insisted that "death" is after all an extraneous factor. If "baptismal resurrection" undergone by some of Paul's readers was *the* great turning point and it lay in the past, then Christians would be rejoicing in a present immortal life, and "death" as Paul has been writing of it would be irrelevant to those already beyond its reach.

We can be pretty sure that this, or something like it, was a teaching enjoying current status at Corinth. Paul would not otherwise have retorted warmly, "Foolish person!" to dispel the aberration. The term *aphrōn* does not imply a person afflicted with madness, or an ignoramus; it is not stupidity but rather a godless attitude (as in Ps. 14:1: "the fool [*aphrōn*] says . . . there is no God" [LXX 13:1]; cf. Luke 12:20) that is in Paul's mind. He finds fault with his interlocutor, who cannot believe how the dead can come to life, because he has left God out of his reckoning.

Yet, Paul avers, it must be so; since Christ was raised *from the dead,* Christians have to die before they can be raised. (The case of the one exceptional class will be deferred until 15:51: not all will die, for Christians who are alive at the parousia will be changed without dying.) Now Paul reasons more simply by taking an illustration from the world of nature (v. 36). A seed is planted in the earth where it "dies"—but its "death" is required in order to lead to germination and new life, which in time produces growth, full development, and fruitage (see John 12:24). As Conzelmann expresses it, the argument makes two points: (a) the necessity of death as the condition of life; and (b) the discontinuity between the present and the future life. Both deductions from the analogy of the wheat grain are directed to the Corinthian scene.

(a) There were those who imagined a resurrection without a preceding death. But this is not a new thought, as Conzelmann alleges, since it seems implicit in 15:12 where it is already stated that Christ is raised from the dead as the firstfruits—and by inference only he so far has been raised. The rest of humankind, including the Corinthian believers, as people-in-Adam, will have to die (15:22).

(b) The element of discontinuity, however, does answer an apparently fresh Corinthian argument. From the natural world Paul reasons that as it is a "naked grain" (*gymnos kokkos*, v. 37) that is sown, the emerging stalk is already clothed with a "body" of the kernel and husk. The Corinthian objection here was to Paul's picture of "body," for they thought in terms of a *dis*embodied spirit as a reality—a concept Paul, in Hebraic fashion, abhors (2 Cor. 5:2–4). There is a similar story in the Jewish literature:

> Queen Cleopatra asked rabbi Meir: "I know . . . the dead will come out of the city (of Jerusalem) like the grass of the earth. But will they rise naked or with clothes? The rabbi replied: The answer is given by the conclusion *a fortiori* [the principle of "how much more"] by taking the case of a grain of wheat. If a grain of wheat was buried naked and comes out of the ground abundantly clothed, how much more will the righteous be dressed in their clothes! (*b. Sanhedrin* 90b)

Paul adds, however, one extra factor, contained in a central phrase:"God gives the grain a body *as he willed*" (*kathōs ēthelēsen*, as in 1 Cor. 12:18) and "to each of the seeds [he gives] *its own body*" (*to idion sōma,* a phrase reminiscent of 15:23, "each in its own turn"). Paul has two strong statements in this text to make against his detractors. First, the principle of "life emerging from death" is in one sense part of the natural order of the farmer's law of sowing and reaping; but at the deeper level, that is, theologically considered, it is a miracle of God to produce life out of death and to give a "new body" (v. 44, a *sōma pneumatikon*) to the elect, as it is God the Creator and preserver of his world that produces the annual miracle of the harvest field (see Ps. 65:9–11, which six times repeats "Thou. . . ," referring to God who is king over creation).

Second, the "body" in which the grain appears is adapted to its new environment not as a seed but as a germinant plant. Paul sustains the argument over the next few verses (39–42), all of which say the same thing (based on Gen. 1:11). Men, animals, birds, fish—all belong to a kingdom of animate life where there are different kinds of bodies corresponding to the habitat of men, animals, birds, and fish. Each species has a body suited to its environment: "A Robin Redbreast in a Cage / Puts all Heaven in a Rage" (Blake).

The foundation of Paul's argument appears firm. God is a God of order and infinite design, with resources of great power to fashion bodies to meet special occasions. Why boggle, then, at the concept of a "supernatural body" (v. 44; Héring's accurate rendering) to replace our present "natural" bodies? To that discussion he now comes. Meanwhile, we can enunciate Paul's principle in a simple epigram: in the world of nature, which is God's world, what is *sown* is not identical with what is *grown*, though it is related to it. God watches over a "dead" seed and in due time it will yield a harvest, not of seeds but of the produce of the field, vineyard, and orchard.

THE PRIORITY OF RESURRECTION

The hinge of Paul's discussion turns on verse 42, "so it will be with the resurrection of the dead," for its purpose is to link the foregoing analogy with the subsequent reply, evoked by the initial question (v. 35: "what kind of body?"). His thought here, however, moves onto a different plane. No longer is he interested in "body" in the natural sense; henceforward "body" will be the human body as the expression par excellence of all that makes a human being unique. It is "the importance of being human" that preoccupies Paul now.

"The 'body' is sown" (v. 42) is a phrase that invites us to consider Paul's teaching on the human body (*sōma*). To us the word relates to our physical frame, but Paul's usage is much more complex. We can see this complexity in 1 Corinthians 6:12–20, on which J. Weiss adds a helpful comment: "The body . . . is not only the material body . . . but the imperishable form of the personality." It stands for the real self, the whole person; for Paul, it seems also to include the element of physicality or embodiment (so R. H. Gundry).[6] What is equally to be stressed is that for Paul there is an ambivalence about the role of the "body," which our present passage illustrates.

Paul assumes, based on Old Testament teaching, that the body as part of God's created order is good (Gen. 1; Ps. 139). As such it is the divinely ordained vehicle of the human spirit; indeed, we may say it *is* the spirit in visible expression representing a person's true self as God's gift of personhood. The Greek term for this notion is *eikōn,* a word Paul employs in 15:49: "As we have borne the *likeness* of the earthly man [Adam], so we shall bear the *likeness* of the man from heaven" (Christ, who expresses the full "selfhood" of God, a reference to v. 47, "the second man is from heaven"). It is difficult to deny an allusion to Christ's pretemporal existence in this latter verse, though J. D. G. Dunn has reopened the issue with such a denial.[7] *Eikōn,* "form," "image," refers, then, to man's unique category (1 Cor. 11:7) as human; it is in this form that the essence—whether of humanity or of deity (in the case of Christ, Col. 1:15; cf. Phil. 2:6)—comes to visible expression, as W. Eltester's full semantic study of the word makes clear.[8]

The obverse side of the coin is that "body," used of man in his or her humanness, is beset by natural limitations. It is "our lowly bodies" (Phil. 3:21) that we now live in and through which we express who we are. Some of these restrictions are part of God's ordering of life. The body is weak, mortal, and subject to decay (Paul's term is "perishable"; vv. 42, 52–54), because, like Adam's, it will return as dust to the earth. The verdict of Genesis 3:19 lies behind verses 47 and 48a where human beings are part of the "man of dust" (NIV "earthly," but this is less expressive).

More seriously, however, the body lies under a judgment sentence because it becomes "an instrument of unrighteousness" (Rom. 6:13). Man as a sinner uses his or her body as a vehicle for transgressing God's command. If we recall that "body" means much more than our physical frame or sensual instincts (as in "bodily sins"), we shall see how Paul has a comprehensive way of calling an individual a sinner when he talks of "presenting" one's body to evil (Rom. 6:19) and then, as a corrective, of presenting one's body to God as a living sacrifice (Rom. 12:1). We might put it simply by remarking that *sōma* is the vehicle that can be either dominated by man's lower nature, his "self" in alienation from God (*sarx*) or put under the control of God's spirit (*pneuma*), for which Paul in this chapter uses the term "glory" (*doxa*: see Conzelmann, who makes this neat distinction). The body as a neutral term has been invaded by *sarx* and now becomes a synonym for man-as-sinner. Only thus can we understand why Paul can hope for "the redemption of our bodies" (Rom. 8:23). And on this basis too we should understand 15:42ff. *at a deeper level.*

Paul vividly portrays "the natural body" (*sōma psychikon*): it is "perishable" since it belongs to an age that is enslaved by evil powers, even if they are on the road to destruction (1 Cor. 2:6); it is capable of dishonor when a person abuses his body (as in Rom. 1:24–32); it is weak in its resistance to the attack of the invading *sarx* (so Paul found in his experience as he cried out for deliverance from "this body of death"—inhabited by sin—since the "flesh" had been welcomed and had taken over; Rom. 7:20–24); it is physically destructible, that is, liable to dissolution in the grave. And all this sad legacy is ours, Paul says, because the "natural" body is stamped with Adam's likeness (v. 49a). Made in God's image, man chose to live independently of his Creator, suffered the defacing of that image as a consequence, and has passed on a twisted nature to his posterity (Gen. 1:26, 27, which goes with Gen. 2:7, in turn quoted in v. 45; Gen. 3:17–24; Gen. 5:3; and we should also remember how Adam's fate is the theme of Paul's Jewish teachers).

The citation of Genesis 2:7 in verse 45 is at the heart of this discussion. "Adam became a living *soul*" (the last word, rendered *psychē* in the Greek Bible, gave Paul the adjective *psychikos* in v. 44: "there is a *natural* body"). Clearly, *psychikos* stands in direct antithesis to *pneumatikos,* as also in verse 44 where the best translation is "supernatural body," since that adjective emphasizes both the resurrection body as a gift of God and its true dignity as the shrine of the Holy Spirit (*pneuma*), as in 1 Corinthians 6:19 and 20. As such the *sōma* is consecrated for divine service and no longer under the dominion of the old order of sin and death. Failing to see that the new age had begun by a transforming of the body, even if the resurrection is still future, had led the Corinthians into serious moral lapses.

This error on their part may help us to account for the argument apparently slipped in as an aside at verse 46: "the spiritual did not come first, but the natural, and after that the spiritual." Conzelmann makes the suggestion that both the wording of verse 44b and the addendum of verse 46 are polemically slanted. Some writers submit that Paul is opposing a type of biblical exegesis, derived from Philo or the Gnostic opponents at Corinth, that argued that the pneumatic takes precedence in time over the physical, just as the creation story in Genesis 1 comes before Genesis 2:7 with its description of Adam as "a living *psychē.*" But others have objected to this, for there is no solid evidence that Paul is working with the myth of a primal man. J. Jeremias[9] has a stronger argument when he takes verse 46 as referring simply to the bodily nature of Christians, which, Paul argues polemically, has first to be "physical"; then at the parousia of Christ believers will receive the "spiritual" body as a gift from God. Paul's opponents wished to discount the physical—or rather, psychical—body altogether, and to concentrate on the "spiritual," which they understood as a body consisting of "spirit." Hence their lax morality in which the human body was treated cavalierly and their claim to be "spiritual" people with a keen desire for spirit-gifts (1 Cor. 14:12). Verses 44b and 45 may indeed be their slogan, quoted in self-justification.

Paul's counterarguments to this are logically arranged:

(a) If verses 44b, 45 are the Corinthians' catchword—since it puts all the stress on "a body possessed of *pneuma*," given by Christ as a life-giving *pneuma,* as they would call it—Paul cites it simply to repel all the wrong ideas that had clustered around it (as in parallel cases of 1 Cor. 6:12ff.; 7:1ff.).[10]

(b) Paul's contrary position is to set the sequence in a new way. According to the Corinthian enthusiasts, first there was Adam, then Christ; once they were in-Adam, but now they are in-Christ, who has raised them to heaven at his resurrection when he became a life-imparting spirit. But Paul's response is that *prior* to Adam who came as a man of dust, Christ was in his premundane existence as "a man of heaven" (v. 47). We all now share in Adam's nature—in all its frailty and finitude—but we shall be remade in the likeness of the heavenly man at the resurrection that is still to come. His opponents said, "There *is* [now] a 'spiritual body' which we received at baptism." Paul counters this with, "We *shall* bear the likeness of the man [who comes at his parousia out] of heaven"; and the only way we can talk of *sōma pneumatikon* is in the implicit future tense: "it is raised a supernatural body" (v. 44a).

(c) The upshot is that we hear in this paragraph two voices articulating two quite diverse anthropologies. The Corinthian self-estimate turns on their claiming a share here and now in the last Adam who has vivified their bodies to transform them into divine beings. Paul marks off (*alla,* "but"; v. 46) his position from this anthropology. The "heavenly man" refers first to the preexistent Lord in his glory. Then Adam was made in that image, which he forfeited. We inherit Adam's liability and loss, but for believers the image is being restored (2 Cor. 3:18; Col. 3:10) until the day when Christ will descend "from heaven" and impart the full image of his own life (Rom. 8:29): "we shall bear (*phoresomen,* a future; the aorist subjunctive *phoresōmen* in P 46, Aleph and the Western texts would be translated as an exhortation, "let us bear"; but the context is clearly against this reading) his likeness then, and only then.

To put the capstone on his argument Paul introduces the next section with a strong asseveration (v. 50): "This I declare" as a "doctrinal statement" (Conzelmann). "Flesh and blood [that is, human beings still indwelling their mortal bodies in all their frailty and still wearing the marks of this old aeon] cannot possess the kingdom of God." Whether Paul is directly writing against a materialistic idea of God's new order or (more likely) against those at Corinth who thought they had already entered the kingdom (1 Cor. 4:8) even though they were still "in the body" (however spiritualized their ideas of bodily existence might be), the conclusion stands. This body essentially belongs to the present aeon and is "perishable." It will die—and if so, it must be raised to inherit the final kingdom; if the living survive until the *terminus ad quem* to which Paul's thought consistently moves, Christ's coming, those bodies will need to be transformed. Either way, the enjoyment of God's kingdom (*regnum Dei,* in contrast to *regnum Christi* which we enter now, according to 1 Cor. 15:23–28) awaits a coming event. Paul's thinking embarks on a new course at this point.

THE NEWNESS OF RESURRECTION

The term "newness" is meant to cover both aspects of the word we use in English: there is new as to quality, and new in regard to time. Both understandings are included in this section (15:51–57). The explanatory word to introduce the theme of newness is "secret" (*mystērion*): "Listen, I tell you a secret," which is both a truth known only to God and yet (paradoxically) revealed to his servants who still have to treat it as mysterious. If verse 50 formed the logical conclusion of Paul's apostolic reasoning, he now claims to have new insight, perhaps in the sense of explaining and amplifying what he had taught the Thessalonians (1 Thess. 4:17).[11] There, at Thessalonica, his schema included a meeting of the departed and living Christians with their Lord, but said nothing of transformation. Here, under pressure of the Corinthian situation, he gains a clearer picture of what is necessary before the final triumph of God is attained. The drama falls into three "acts":

(a) Death will not come to "all" (Christians), for there will be a generation to survive until the end. But even they will need to undergo change (unlike what his readers were thinking with their hope pinned on a baptismal resurrection in this life). The time factor, hinted at in 15:23, is now clarified (v. 52): "in a flash, in the twinkling of an eye, at the last trumpet." The last-named is familiar in the apocalyptic expectation of the end time (Matt. 24:31;

1 Thess. 4:16; cf. Rev. 8:2–13; 11:15–19; 4 Ezra 6:23; Sib. Or. 4.173f.). "Last" does not suggest the last in a series of trumpet blasts, but the sound to usher in the end (as in "last enemy" of 15:26). The end will come swiftly and (apparently) without warning.

(b) At the final trumpet call two classes of people will be (simultaneously?) affected. "The (Christian) dead will be raised"; this sentence spells out Paul's word of consolation to those of his readers who, like the Thessalonians (1 Thess. 4:13–18), may have been distressed over the fate of their departed loved ones and friends. The problem has a sharp edge if they had been told that believers were immortal and that death would present no problem. The second group is involved in the promise, which is equally a requirement (we learn that in v. 51, which has "we shall *all* be changed," with a variety of textual variations): "We shall be changed." The following verb, "must" (v. 53), carries apocalyptic overtones, that is, it is a necessity dictated by the eschatological need for those who would enter the kingdom, whose door is barred to "flesh and blood" (i.e., frail humanity belonging to this age, as in Matt. 16:17, and possibly Gal. 1:16; Heb. 2:14).

The living church that survives to the parousia (among which Paul may well have numbered himself—at least until 2 Cor. 4:13–5:10 was written and possibly until the crisis of 2 Cor. 1:8ff.) will be transformed by the assuming of a "supernatural body" (going back to v. 44).

Paul amplifies this "change," which he will develop considerably at 2 Corinthians 5:2–4 by the thought of the "putting on" of immortality as a covering, so transmuting the believer's earthly "form." The apostle evidently conceived that new life as nothing short of Christ's risen being, his "body of glory" (Phil. 3:21), which is already taking shape in the Christian (Gal. 4:19; 2 Cor. 3:18; Eph. 4:24) but which at the parousia will *appear in visible expression*. We recall the teaching on *eikōn*, "image," as the coming to visible perception of that inner core which constitutes a person's being. It is exactly parallel to what Paul writes (in Rom. 8:19) of creation's yearning for "the sons of God to be revealed."

The "supernatural body" granted at this time has all the marks that reverse the sorry train of events that lead from Adam. In effect, perishability and mortality, the legacy of the man of dust, give way to their opposites. In fact, this is no accident for Paul. The new life marks the transition from the old Adamic order of sin and death to the new age of "imperishability" (*aphtharsia*, a term suited to the deceased whose bodies have long since decayed and gone to dust) and "immortality" (*athanasia*, a term taken by J. Jeremias[12] to have special reference to the living who will exchange their "having to die" for an entrée into God's presence without dying). Of this new age, prophecy (Isa. 25:8; Hos. 13:14) had already spoken, and Paul freely cites the texts in a composite and unusual form:

> Death has been swallowed up in victory.
> Where, O death, is your victory?
> Where, O death, is your sting?

It is clear that Paul is attracted to the catchword "victory" (found in the Aquila and Theodotion versions of Isa. 25 as *eis nikos*, "to victory," to render the Hebrew "for ever"). Hosea 13:14 has in the Hebrew, "O death, where are your plagues? O Sheol, where is your destruction?"; Paul uses and revises this verse because of its opening apostrophe, "O death," and its translation of "destruction" as "sting" (*kentron* in LXX). He finds it a useful lead-in to his next line: "the sting of death is sin." It is just as obvious that Paul has gone to the Isaiah passage because in both Hebrew and Greek the verb is "swallow up," "devour," a verb that plays an important role in his parallel treatment of the resurrection hope of 2 Corinthians 5:4 (see earlier, ch. 6, p. 103).

(c) The link terms (sin—law—death) in Romans 5:12ff. explain their presence in verses 56 and 57. The logic in both texts is clear and incisive. "The law" in Paul's teaching functions in different ways according to the context where it is used. He can write of the law (usually connoting the "law of Moses" in the Old Testament) as God-given and ordained for human well-being; so it is "holy . . . and the commandment is holy, just and good" (Rom. 7:12). At the other extreme, it cannot impart righteousness and give life with God (Gal. 3:21); and in Paul's severest statement it has become a deadly instrument leading to condemnation (2 Cor. 3:6). The ruling idea throughout Paul's discussion is found in the use to which the law is put. The regime of "law" was necessary on account of human extremity and was an interlude "until Christ came" (Gal. 3:23, 24). Law gave a definition and focus to wrongdoing (Rom. 4:15) and so paved the way for the gospel. But in so doing the law by its very nature as suggesting a "contractual" or "transactional" relationship with God to those men and women who were "weak" (see Rom. 8:3: the law is impossible to help such people because of the *sarx,* which perverts and disables the law) acted as an incentive or goad to sin. It set a standard either too high for unaided human attainment or too dangerous by promoting pride when human beings *did* manage to achieve success in keeping it (Phil. 3:6). On both counts, as a work of self-help leading to merit-religion or as a ground for boasting, the law has turned into our enemy. It showed "the power of sin," revealing man as a sinner whether he is a law-breaker or a self-sufficient "religious" person. Sin was able to invade human life through man's inherent frailty as "flesh" (*sarx*), and the result is "death."

We may suppose that, as Paul has used "death" in its physical aspect up to this point, this will be his meaning at verse 56. But "the sting" of which he writes, drawn from Hosea 13:14 as we saw, perhaps has a deeper meaning. It is the penalty of sin, not only in that we share mortality with the animals as a biological necessity, but we are "doomed to die" on account of our sin (Rom. 6:23). Death has become the "sacrament of sin"; it is the outward and visible sign of a spiritual dis-grace.

In a significant turning point, however, a new hope is heralded and a fresh start offered to men and women in the new world opened by God's grace in Christ. So Paul's last word is one of victory (v. 57, comparable with Rom. 7:25).

Verse 58 stands as a stirring conclusion to the entire chapter and an exhortation to turn these kerygmatic truths (Conzelmann)— summed up in the hope of the gospel as it embraces the future— into practical effect. This train of thought is in the typically Pauline manner. In light of what God has done and the church's new life in the risen Christ whose triumph, both present and future, is called "the work of the Lord," a call to perseverance and service rings out. Soteriology, in Paul, always carries an ethical appeal. And in this context, since Paul has insisted at the beginning that the Corinthians remain committed to the gospel (15:1, 2), it is fitting to close on that same note. "Let nothing move you" to leave the apostolic teaching. The assurance goes with the summons that as his readers in staying true to Paul's gospel will not have believed "in vain," so their Christian service will not be an empty (*kenos*) thing. (See 15:14: "our preaching is empty [*kenon*] and your faith is empty [*kene*]" for the play on this word.) So Paul's final shot adds yet one more item to the list of Christian convictions that evaporate into thin air—if Christ's raising is not a sure and certain confidence. [13] Both Paul's ministry (1 Cor. 15:10; Phil. 2:16) and the Corinthians' labor as Christ's witnesses in the world have no meaning without the resurrection hope.

CHAPTER NINE

POSTSCRIPT

In some few closing paragraphs we may take a backward glance across the road by which we have traveled. We took as a starting place the apostle's dual attitude toward this congregation at Corinth. He loved them as their human founder and father (1 Cor. 3:10; 4:15); yet he was concerned for their state as a company of Christians in danger of succumbing to many false hopes and erroneous ways. They were divided over leadership and were blighted by party rivalry. They entertained serious doubts about ethical matters on which Paul had the clearest convictions—especially in the realm of personal sexual morality and the church's relationship to the surrounding world. Their worship was sadly disfigured, both in the public assembly and at the Lord's Supper meal. Their attitudes were characterized by "pride" and unbridled "freedom" that bordered on license in the name of a claim to privatized religious experience, esoteric "knowledge" (*gnōsis*), and flamboyant manifestations of "spirit power."

Yet at the root of all these symptoms was a festering malady. Paul identifies this trouble as doctrinal. In specific terms: (*i*) They failed to appreciate and live by the lordship of the once crucified, now risen Christ. (*ii*) They cherished a defective eschatology according to which their initial response to the gospel in baptism was understood as a "being raised with Christ," a rite of passage into the kingdom claimed as present now in its fullness (1 Cor. 4:8). Thereby they came to denigrate any future expectation of resurrection. (*iii*) Their flush of new life in the Spirit gave them a desire to practice spontaneous, energetic, and uncontrolled worship.

Paul has to offer in these four chapters specific countermeasures and corrective teaching. In so doing, he paints for the Corinthians—and for us, as we seek to apply these matters as relevantly as we can to the church of our own time—certain cameo pictures of what a "healthy" church" would look like:

(a) It would be a church that rejoiced in the "gifts of the Spirit" on which a true evaluation was placed as these "spiritual energies" were seen as God's "gifts-in-grace" (*charismata*) for the well-being of the entire community. The dynamism of the Spirit will be valued, but not to the exclusion of good order, worthy styles of worship, attractive decorum, and, above all, never to a betrayal of Christ's rule as Lord, the "crown rights of the redeemer" over his people.

(b) So a vital church at worship will seek to please God, to cultivate the partnership (*koinōnia*) of love that brings all the members together in mutual respect and interrelated caring, and to keep an eye open for its witness to the contemporary world.

(c) The benchmark of Paul's churchly teaching is "the gospel," enshrined in one early creed and *paradosis,* tradition, which must be allowed to regulate the congregation's life when it is tempted to be drawn aside to subjective preferences and individual foibles. "Christ crucified and raised" stands at the center, with implications that radiate out to touch the periphery of all that the church attempts in worship, common life, and service.

(d) The "healthy church" will anticipate God's future with hope, knowing that while Christians have begun their life-in-Christ and the Holy Spirit has come as a "first installment," there is more yet to be known and explored of God's love. This life-in-Christ, richly endowed and privileged as it is, is still hampered by our mortal weaknesses, and enemies beset us. But the last word is with God, whose kingdom will come at length and whose sure purposes are as undefeatable as the victory that was once gained in the resurrection of his Son. The future will unpack the full significance of that triumphant event, and turn our present hope into glorious reality.

ENDNOTES

N.B. Commentaries used in the text are not always listed here. The commentators' names that do appear refer to their own works ad loc. in abbreviated form. See Bibliography for details, including full references to journal articles cited.

INTRODUCTION

1. On Paul's relations with Corinth see R. P. Martin, *New Testament Foundations*, 2:170–87; and for Corinth see S. E. Johnson, "Paul in the Wicked City of Corinth," 59–67; W. A. Meeks, *The First Urban Christians. The Social World of the Apostle Paul*, 47–49; J. Murphy-O'Connor, *St. Paul's Corinth. Texts and Archaeology*.

2. See G. Theissen, *The Social Setting of Pauline Christianity: Essays on Corinth*, 69–119; Meeks, *First Urban Christians*, 117–25.

3. 1 Clement 47:3 reads: "With true inspiration he [Paul] charged you concerning himself and Cephas and Apollos, because even then you had made yourselves partisans" (Lake's trans.). On this text see C. K. Barrett, *Essays on Paul*, 5.

4. S. Neill, *The Christian Faith Today*, 170.

5. Quoted in David C. Watson, *I Believe in the Church*, 13.

6. K. Barth, as quoted in J. J. von Allmen, *Worship: Its Theology and Practice*, 13.

CHAPTER ONE

1. J. Goldingay, *The Church and the Gifts of the Spirit*, 5; E. Käsemann, "Ministry and the Community in the New Testament," in *Essays on New Testament Themes*, 64f.

2. J. Koenig, *Charismata: God's Gifts for God's People*, 107. So, too, D. M. Smith, "Glossolalia and Other Spiritual Gifts in a NT Perspective," 311; D. W. B. Robinson, "*Charismata* versus *Pneumatika*. Paul's Method of Discussion," 49–55.

3. E. Käsemann, *Commentary on Romans*, 226.

4. See W. Kramer, *Christ, Lord, Son of God*, 65–107 (secs. 15a–23g).

5. A summary of possibilities of interpreting 12:3 is given in R. P. Martin, *The Worship of God*, 175–78; see also B. A. Pearson, *The Pneumatikos-Psychikos Terminology in 1 Corinthians*, 47–50, and J. M. Bassler, "1 Cor. 12:3—Curse and

Confession in Context," 415–21. Pearson's argument is of merit because he indicates a weakness in W. Schmithals's proposal that the utterance "Jesus be cursed" was a gnosticizing one thereby separating the earthly, suffering Jesus from the heavenly, passionless Christ (for this distinction see Irenaeus, *Adv. Haer.* 1.26.1). "The key to a proper understanding of 1 Corinthians 12:1–3 is the recognition that it belongs to the whole context in chapters 12–14." The cry of 12:3, taken as ecstatic speech, is understood by Pearson as a throwback to the Corinthians' pagan past when, it may be, the Corinthians "vented their curses against Jesus Christ"; or even, Pearson suggests, Paul's own contrived antithesis to the common Christian confession to shock his enthusiastic readers who believed ecstatic speech was an infallible mark of "spiritual" Christianity.

The drawback in this reconstruction is the difficulty in regarding all ecstatic speaking per se as evil and in thinking that Paul "invented" the cry, or even that the cry was hypothetical (Pearson, 49). In spite of Pearson's disavowal (p. 48), the verse does seem to set in antithesis two conflicting confessions (cf. 2 Cor. 11:4). This is the issue at stake, as C. K. Barrett (*The First Epistle to the Corinthians,* 279) remarks, "Not the manner but the content of ecstatic speech determines its authenticity."

D. E. Aune is another interpreter of 1 Cor. 12:2, 3 who thinks that the exclamation "Jesus be cursed!" was not uttered within the Corinthian community but is a "hypothetical Pauline construct" created as an antithesis to the credal cry, "Jesus is Lord!" (*Prophecy in Early Christianity and the Ancient Mediterranean World,* 256f.). This is most improbable, even granting that Paul (in v. 2) refers to the Corinthians' pagan religious experience. The mention of that verse most naturally accounts for the way some Christians at Corinth were expressing their disdain of Jesus, and that leaves open the question of what motivated them to do so.

6. Barrett, *First Epistle to the Corinthians,* 281.

7. E. Schweizer, *The Holy Spirit,* 126.

8. F. F. Bruce, *1 and 2 Corinthians,* 119.

9. A. Bittlinger, *Gifts and Graces,* 20–22; cf. Bittlinger, *Gifts and Ministries,* 20ff.

10. J. W. MacGorman, *The Gifts of the Spirit,* 35.

11. W. Baird, *The Corinthian Church—A Biblical Approach to Urban Culture,* 139.

12. Bruce, *1 and 2 Corinthians,* 119.

13. See Pearson, *The Pneumatikos—Psychikos Terminology,* 44–50, and C. K. Barrett, *Essays on Paul,* 7–14, who analyzes the different senses of *sophia* in Paul's usage.

14. E. E. Ellis, "'Wisdom' and 'Knowledge' in 1 Corinthians," in *Prophecy and Hermeneutic in Early Christianity,* 61.

15. Bittlinger, *Gifts and Graces,* 37.

16. D. Hill, *New Testament Prophecy,* 128, 131.

17. Barrett, *First Epistle to the Corinthians,* 286.

CHAPTER TWO

1. J. Denney, "The Superlative Way," in *The Way Everlasting,* 152.

2. J. A. T. Robinson, *The Body. A Study in Pauline Theology.*

3. S. Kim, *The Origin of Paul's Gospel*.

4. So G. J. Cuming, "*Epotisthēmen*: 1 Corinthians 12:13," 283–85.

5. E. Käsemann, "Ministry and Community," in *Essays on New Testament Themes*, 76.

6. E. Best, *One Body in Christ*, 103; cf. W. Baird, *The Corinthian Church*, 144.

7. E. Schweizer, "The Church as the Missionary Body of Christ," 1ff. especially p. 5.

8. R. Banks, *Paul's Idea of Community*.

9. C. K. Barrett, *The First Epistle to the Corinthians*, referring to A. Fridrichsen, *The Apostle and His Message*.

10. For the present writer's understanding of Ephesians 4:16, see *The Family and the Fellowship*, 69–72.

11. G. Iber, "Zum Verständnis von I Cor. 12, 31," 43–52; see on this G. D. Fee, "Tongues—Least of the Gifts? Some Exegetical Observations on 1 Corinthians 12–14," 3–14.

12. A. Bittlinger, *Gifts and Graces*, 73.

13. D. L. Baker, "The Interpretation of I Corinthians 12–14," 224–34.

14. M.-A. Chevallier, *Esprit de Dieu, Paroles d'Hommes*, 163, 159, 158.

15. O. Wischmeyer, *Der höchste Weg. Das 13. Kapitel des 1. Korintherbriefes*, 32.

16. E. Käsemann, *Leib and Leib Christi*, 170; cf. W. J. Bartling, "The Congregation of Christ: A Charismatic Body," 67–80.

17. Käsemann, "Ministry and Community," 71, 72.

18. E. Käsemann, *Commentary on Romans*, 333.

CHAPTER THREE

1. O. Wischmeyer, *Der höchste Weg. Das 13. Kapitel des 1. Korintherbriefes*, 163ff.

2. G. von Rad, "Die Vorgeschichte der Gattung von 1. Kor. 13, 4–7," in *Geschichte und Altes Testament*, 153–68.

3. Wischmeyer (*Der höchste Weg*, 233) regards verses 1–3 as a *Wertepriamel*, that is, a literary schema that contrasts one ethical value with a series of other values and finds it to be superior. But this is to be questioned since *agapē* is not one of the *pneumatika* but the essential accompaniment of all the spirit-gifts.

4. A. von Harnack, *The Mission and Expansion of Christianity*, 1:148f.

5. K. Barth, *Church Dogmatics* IV/2, 824–40.

6. H. Riesenfeld, "Note sur I Cor. 13," 2f.

7. Wischmeyer, *Der höchste Weg*, p. 73.

8. K. Beyschlag, "Clemens Romanus," 34, cited in M. Hengel, *The Charismatic Leader and his Followers*, 74; G. Theissen, *The Social Setting of Pauline Christianity: Essays on Corinth*, 40–54.

9. G. Bornkamm, *Early Christian Experience*, 181.

10. H. Riesenfeld, "Vorbildliches Martyrium," in *Donum Gentilicum. NT Studies in Honour of David Daube*, 210–14. See the discussion of the textual problem in G. Zuntz, *The Text of the Epistles*, 35ff.

11. Bornkamm, 190 n. 16.

12. A. Fridrichsen, *The Problem of Miracle in Primitive Christianity*, 145.

13. Wischmeyer, *Der höchste Weg*, 92 n. 238.

14. W. Barclay, *New Testament Words*, 196–98.
15. H. Braun, *"perpereuomai,"* in *The Theological Dictionary of the New Testament*, 6:93.
16. Wischmeyer, *Der höchste Weg*, 105.
17. W. Schrage, "Leid, Kreuz und Eschaton," 141–75.
18. K. Barth, *The Resurrection of the Dead*, 84.
19. Wischmeyer, *Der höchste Weg*, 162.
20. For details, see R. P. Martin, "A Suggested Exegesis of I Corinthians 13:13," 119f.
21. Though this point can be exaggerated; N. Johansson, "I Cor. xiii and I Cor. xiv," 386: "What Paul is describing is a definite historical figure, the Christ of the Gospel tradition." C. Senft regards this view as "exegetically indefensible" (*La première épître*, 172).
22. J. Denney, *The Way Everlasting*, 163.
23. L. B. Smedes, *Love Within Limits*, 126.
24. Denney, *Way Everlasting*, 161.
25. Wischmeyer, *Der höchste Weg*, 230–33; for the eschatological motifs in this passage see S. Pedersen, "Agape—der eschatologische Hauptbegriff bei Paulus," in *Die paulinische Literatur und Theologie*, ed. Sigfred Pedersen, 159–86. On this essay, cf. Wischmeyer, p. 9.

CHAPTER FOUR

1. P. F. Bradshaw, *Daily Prayer in the Early Church*, 20.
2. E. Schweizer, *Church Order in the New Testament*, 185 (22f.).
3. E. Schweizer, "Worship in the New Testament," 295.
4. J. Héring, *The First Epistle of Saint Paul to the Corinthians*, 4, 112, 114. This attendance of the entire church in one place is an important factor when social conditions at the Corinthian agape and eucharist are considered. It tends to get overlooked in G. Theissen's essay, "Social Integration and Sacramental Activity: An Analysis of 1 Cor. 11:17–34," in *The Social Setting of Pauline Christianity*, 145–74.
5. R. J. Neuhaus, *Freedom for Ministry*, 125, 127, 128 for following citations in the text.
6. M.-A. Chevallier, *Esprit de Dieu, Paroles d'Hommes*, 172.
7. J. Goldingay, *The Church and the Gifts of the Spirit*, 18–21.
8. J. W. MacGorman, *The Gifts of the Spirit: An Exposition of I Corinthians 12–14*, 81.
9. J. D. G. Dunn, *Jesus and the Spirit*, 245. On the "type" of speech referred to in chapter 14 see C. G. Williams, *Tongues of the Spirit, A Study of Pentecostal Glossolalia and Related Phenomena*, ch. 2. He argues cogently for "ecstatic" tongues. The coincidence of reported glossolalia with a known language is explained, with Felicitas D. Goodman (*Speaking in Tongues: A Cross-Cultural Study of Glossolalia*, 148–51), as a matter of statistical probability, namely, that glossolalic sounds will, given enough examples, bear resemblance to meaningful words in some human language: cf. Williams, pp. 183–89.
10. J. Héring, *First Corinthians*, 145.

11. J. D. G. Dunn, *Jesus and the Spirit*, 229.

12. W. J. Hollenweger, *The Pentecostals*, 344.

13. Dunn, *Jesus and the Spirit*, 232 (printed in italics).

14. E. Käsemann, "Sentences of Holy Law in the New Testament," in *New Testament Questions of Today*, 66–81.

15. M. E. Thrall, *I and II Corinthians*, 99. See H. Wayne House, "Tongues and the Mystery Religions of Corinth," 135–50 for the comment that in verse 4 Paul's statement is conciliatory, "merely conced[ing] a point here for argument." H. Chadwick ("All Things to All Men," 261–75) has effectively shown that this was Paul's strategy in handling the delicate situation at Corinth.

16. Dunn, *Jesus and the Spirit*, 238.

17. Williams, *Tongues of the Spirit*, 231.

18. Williams, *Tongues of the Spirit*, 213. The nursery-words of Isaiah 28:10 (Heb. *ṣaw lā-ṣāw, qaw lā-qāw*) is not glossalalic speech, even if the following verse is cited by Paul.

19. Chevallier, *Esprit de Dieu, Paroles d'Hommes*, 149 n. 4. This estimate is true only if we qualify it. *Lalein* is used of the prophetic speech but there is then a direct object of the verb (14:3); where there is not, *lalein* means a glossolalic utterance.

20. On Paul's use of the OT here see E. E. Ellis (*Paul's Use of the Old Testament*, 107–12) who suggests the presence of a fragment of Christian anti-Jewish polemic. This understanding is seen in J. M. Sweet, "A Sign for Unbelievers," 240–57.

21. Thrall, *I and II Corinthians*, 100.

22. The verb "to be" in 14:22 ("Tongues are [*eisin*] for a sign") could very well carry the exegetical sense: "Tongues represent, stand for."

23. Schweizer, *Church Order in the New Testament*, 101–3 (7 1, m).

24. In a way similar to Paul's appropriation of Zechariah 14:9 in reference to the universal "Lord" identified with the exalted Jesus, see D. R. de Lacey, "'One Lord' in Pauline Christology," in *Christ the Lord: Studies in Christology presented to Donald Guthrie*, ed. H. H. Rowdon, 196–203.

CHAPTER FIVE

1. Cf. J. D. G. Dunn, *Jesus and the Spirit*, 266; J. Painter, "Paul and the *Pneumatikoi* at Corinth," in *Paul and Paulinism*, ed. M. D. Hooker and S. G. Wilson, 237–50; and R. Scroggs, "Paul and the Eschatological Woman," 283–303.

2. A. Robertson and A. Plummer, *A Critical and Exegetical Commentary on the First Epistle of St. Paul to the Corinthians*, 320; see my discussion in "Some Reflections on New Testament Hymns," in *Christ the Lord: Studies in Christology presented to Donald Guthrie*, ed. H. H. Rowdon, 37f.

3. A. C. Thiselton, "The 'Interpretation' of Tongues," 15–36.

4. D. Hill, *New Testament Prophecy*, 137f.

5. I have suggested that the prophets contributed Christ-hymns, such as Philippians 2:6–11 and 1 Timothy 3:16, as part of this ministry of upbuilding in terms of offering praise to the exalted Lord (cf. my "Reflections on New Testa-

ment Hymns," 132–36) and inculcating "healthy teaching" on his saving work. See next note.

6. Hill, *New Testament Prophecy*, 128.

7. J. Héring, *The First Epistle of Saint Paul to the Corinthians*, 152.

8. U. B. Müller, *Prophetie und Predigt im Neuen Testament*, 27 (cited in Hill, *New Testament Prophecy*, 134).

9. See D. E. Aune, *Prophecy in Early Christianity and the Ancient Mediterranean World*, 219–22.

10. G. Friedrich, *"prophētēs,"* in *The Theological Dictionary of the New Testament*, 6:851; Hill, *New Testament Prophecy*, 133; Aune, *Prophecy*, 402 n. 36, but cf. p. 222 for a slightly different sense involving the community.

11. Dunn, *Jesus and the Spirit*, 233–36.

12. The verb *mainomai* suggests not simply mental disorder ("you are mad") but demonic invasion ("you are possessed"). See N. I. Engelsen, *Glossolalia and Other Forms of Inspired Speech According to 1 Corinthians 12–14*, 6, and Gingrich-Danker, *A Greek-English Lexicon*, 486 on v. 23.

13. Robertson-Plummer, *Commentary on First Corinthians*, 328; for an eccentric view of 1 Corinthians 14:39 see C. D. Isabell, "Glossolalia and Propheteialalia: A Study of I Cor. 14," 15–22.

14. J. Koenig, *Charismata. God's Gifts for God's People*, 174.

15. G. Zuntz, *The Text of the Epistles*, 17; see now E. E. Ellis's full note on the textual issues, "The Silenced Wives of Corinth (I Cor. 14:34–5)," in B. M. Metzger Festschrift *New Testament Textual Criticism*, ed. E. J. Epp and G. D. Fee, 213–20.

16. A. Bittlinger, *Gifts and Graces*, 113, 114. He regards this attempt as a failure since 14:33–36 is at odds with 11:5.

17. R. Scroggs, "Paul and the Eschatological Woman," 294ff.

18. J. W. MacGorman, *The Gifts of the Spirit: An Exposition of I Corinthians 12–14*, 113.

19. J. N. Sevenster, *Paul and Seneca*, 198.

20. Not even Genesis 3:16, a text usually appealed to, says anything about a woman's silence. The term "law" (*nomos*) carries a wide range of meanings, as we can see from the use of *nomos* in 14:21 to refer to Isaiah.

21. J. B. Hurley (*Man and Woman in Biblical Perspective*, 185–94) draws upon Grudem's work, since published as *The Gift of Prophecy in 1 Corinthians*; see especially pp. 245–55.

22. M. E. Thrall, *I and II Corinthians*, 102.

23. Dunn, *Jesus and the Spirit*, 235; see too W. A. Grudem on "judging the prophets," in "A Response to Gerhard Dautzenberg on I Cor. 12:10," 253–70, and *Gift of Prophecy*, 58–67 (cf. pp. 263–88). Grudem argues that "the others" (14:32) relates to the entire congregation and the verb *diakrinō* means no more than that "the congregation would simply evaluate the prophecy and form opinions about it." We may query whether this way of describing prophecy does justice to the wording of 14:3 and 4.

24. K. Stendahl, *The Bible and the Role of Women*, 32ff.

25. Or, specifically as E. E. Ellis argues ("The Silenced Wives," 218), the women seem to have been involved in publicly "testing" their own husbands' prophetic messages, and asserting a teaching role over them.

A similar view is taken by John E. Toews in "The Role of Women in the

Church: A Pauline Perspective," 25–35, especially 30f. Toews sees the injunction to silence and subordination as of limited appeal to a special circumstance at
Corinth, namely, that the women were "testing" their husbands in the assembly.
He believes Paul's advice is aimed at solving marital disputes in public and at
having women discuss prophetic oracles at home.

26. "Godless chatter" of 2 Timothy 2:16 is evidently how the Pastor regards
this false teaching, and it is possible that the women of 1 Timothy 5:11–15 who
"say things they ought not to" are the originators of these ideas against which
Timothy is warned (1 Tim. 6:20, 21). If 1 Timothy 4:1–3 is part of the same
teaching, we may find here how women's claim to be celibate teachers—a per-
sistent idea in the second-century Asia Minor church (see Dennis R. MacDonald,
The Legend and the Apostle, 79–81 for the list of women prophetesses)—found
support in their cognate claim to be living in the new age of the realized kingdom
where encratite ways of living mirrored their "freedom" (see W. L. Lane,
"1 Timothy iv.1–3. An Early Instance of Over-Realized Eschatology?" 164–
67).

27. For the view that "the Corinthians appear then to have held that they
were as angels in their new eschatological existence," see A. T. Lincoln, *Paradise
Now and Not Yet*, 34ff.

CHAPTER SIX

1. F. F. Bruce, *1 and 2 Corinthians*, 137.

2. See G. Zuntz, *The Text of the Epistles*, 254.

3. J. Munck, "Paulus tanquam abortivus," in *New Testament Essays in Memory
of T. W. Manson*, ed. A. J. B. Higgins, 180–93.

4. Th. Boman, "Paulus abortivus (I Kor. 15,8)," 46–50.

5. A. Schweitzer, *The Mysticism of Paul the Apostle*, 93.

6. J. Schniewind, "Die Leugnung der Auferstehung in Korinth," in
Nachgelassene Reden und Aufsätze, ed. E. Kahler, 110–39. But this is by no means a
universal opinion—even if the present writer believes it still to be the most
adequate explanation of all the Corinthian phenomena. See now R. McL. Wilson,
"Gnosis at Corinth," in *Paul and Paulinism*, ed. M. D. Hooker and S. G. Wilson,
102–14; and A. J. M. Wedderburn, "The Problem of the Denial of the Resurrection," 229–41.

7. W. Baird, *The Corinthian Church—A Biblical Approach to Urban Culture*,
164.

8. W. Künneth, *The Theology of the Resurrection*, 249ff.

9. On this point see M. Hengel, *Acts and the History of Earliest Christianity*,
71–80.

10. K. Wegenast, *Das Verständnis der Tradition bei Paulus und in den Deuteropaulinen*, 52–70; for the view that takes verses 3–7a as a unity see J. Murphy-
O'Connor ("Tradition and Redaction in I Cor. 15:3–7," 583–89), who argues
against a majority view that has raised objections to the meaning of verses 6 and 7
in the credo. See J. H. Schütz, *Paul and the Anatomy of Apostolic Authority*, 95f.

11. J. Kloppenborg, "An Analysis of the Pre-Pauline Formula I Cor. 15:3b–
5 in the Light of Some Recent Literature," 351–67.

12. E. E. Ellis, *Paul's Use of the Old Testament*, 22.

13. B. M. Metzger, "A Suggestion Concerning the Meaning of I Cor. xv. 4b," 118–23; B. Lindars, *New Testament Apologetic*, 59–72.

14. W. Marxsen, *The Resurrection of Jesus of Nazareth*, 80–87.

15. K. Stendahl, *Paul among Jews and Gentiles*, 7–23.

16. R. P. Martin, *Reconciliation: A Study of Paul's Theology*, 24–31.

17. S. Kim, *The Origin of Paul's Gospel*, 51–66

18. H. C. G. Moule, *The Cross and the Spirit*, 55.

19. D. M. Baillie, *God was in Christ*, 114–18.

20. E. Güttgemanns, *Der leidende Apostel und sein Herr*, 74f.

21. A. Schlatter, *Paulus, der Bote Jesu*, 405.

22. E. Brunner, *The Mediator*, 563.

23. E. Lohse, *Colossians and Philemon*, 131.

24. See *The Gnostic Treatise on Resurrection from Nag Hammadi*, ed. and trans. B. Layton, 15, 17; and 56–65 for commentary.

25. J. H. Moulton and N. Turner, *A Grammar of the New Testament Greek*, 3:228; Schütz (*Paul and the Anatomy of Apostolic Authority*, 90f.) sees a measure of agreement at this point between Paul and the enthusiasts. But they profess to have more than *hope*; they are living in a realized kingdom.

CHAPTER SEVEN

1. C. K. Barrett, *The First Epistle to the Corinthians*, 350; see W. Dykstra, "I Cor. 15:20–28: An Essential Part of Paul's Argument Against those who Deny the Resurrection," 195–211; K. A. Plank, "Resurrection Theology: The Corinthian Controversy Re-examined," 41–54.

2. O. Cullmann, *Christ and Time*[2] and *Salvation in History*; W. G. Kümmel, *Theology of the New Testament*; G. E. Ladd, *A Theology of the New Testament*.

3. E. Lohmeyer, *Der Brief an die Philipper*, 96; cf. idem, *Kyrios Jesus: Eine Untersuchung zu Phil. 2, 5–11*, 43, referring to Revelation 1:18.

4. C. E. B. Cranfield, "The Interpretation of I Peter iii.19 and iv.6," 369–72.

5. See O. Cullmann, *The Earliest Christian Confessions*.

6. C. F. D. Moule, *The Birth of the New Testament*, 149: "Always at moments of Christian worship, time and space are obliterated and the worshipping Church on earth is one in eternity with the church in the heavenly places." This fine statement, however, needs some adjustment to account for the earthly church's existence *in via* and not yet having reached its goal *in patria*.

7. E. Schweizer, "Der Glaube an Jesus den 'Herrn' in seiner Entwicklung von den ersten Nachfolgern bis zur hellenistischen Gemeinde," 7–21, especially 13ff.

8. Barrett, *First Corinthians*, 356; K. Barth, *The Resurrection of the Dead*, 162f.; F. C. Burkitt, "On I Corinthians xv.26," 384f.

9. O. Cullmann, *The Christology of the New Testament*, 293f.; see too J. F. Jansen, "I Cor. 15:24–28," in *Texts and Testaments*, ed. W. E. March, 173–97.

10. K. C. Thompson, "I Corinthians 15,29 and Baptism for the Dead," 647–59.

11. M. Rissi, *Die Taufe für die Toten*, 54.

12. M. Raeder, "Vikariastaufe in I Cor. 15,29?" 258–60; J. Jeremias, "'Flesh and Blood cannot Inherit the Kingdom of God' (I Cor. xv.50)," 151–59.

13. Rissi, *Die Taufe*, 85f.
14. F. Godet, *Commentary on I Corinthians*, ad loc. See G. R. Beasley-Murray, *Baptism in the New Testament*, 185–92 for a review of other possibilities.
15. J. C. O'Neill, "I Corinthians 15:29," 310, 311.
16. See A. J. Malherbe, "The Beasts at Ephesus," 71–80 for evidence of a nonliteral sense.
17. Cited in Conzelmann, *I Corinthians*, ad loc.
18. G. S. Duncan, *St. Paul's Ephesian Ministry*; see R. P. Martin, *Colossians and Philemon*, 26–28 for the life-setting.
19. K. Barth, *The Epistle to the Philippians*, 38.
20. The keyword *gnōsis* suggests that Paul is indeed polemicizing against the Corinthians who claimed esoteric knowledge (8:1), but (Paul remarks) they lack true "knowledge" of God in the Old Testament meaning of that phrase, that is, vital fellowship with God (cf. *da'at 'elohim* in, e.g., Hosea 4:1–6; 6:6).

CHAPTER EIGHT

1. W. Schmithals, *Gnosticism in Corinth*, 169f.; E. Schweizer, *"pneuma,"* in *The Theological Dictionary of the New Testament*, 6:420f.
2. J. Schniewind, "Die Leugnung der Auferstehung in Korinth," in *Nachgelassene Reden und Aufsätze*, ed. Erich Kahler, 110–39, especially p. 130; E. Brandenburger, *Adam und Christus*, 73.
3. J. Jeremias, "'Flesh and Blood cannot Inherit the Kingdom of God' (I Cor. xv.50)," 151–59.
4. E. Schweizer, *"sarx,"* in *The Theological Dictionary of the New Testament*, 7:128f.
5. K. Usami, "How are the Dead Raised?" 468–93.
6. See the full discussion in R. H. Gundry, *SŌMA in Biblical Theology: with Emphasis on Pauline Anthropology*.
7. J. D. G. Dunn, *Christology in the Making*, 107–10. Dunn wishes to use the principle of verse 46: "the spiritual" is not first, but the earthly, then [comes] "the spiritual" in a christological way, so denying that Christ's role as ultimate Adam may be taken back to his pretemporal existence. Rather, Dunn says, the idea of Christ-as-last-Adam belongs only to his resurrection state. But this line of reasoning (a) takes verse 46 to be a christological reference, whereas it is better construed as an anthropological description of the sequence Paul wants to insist on: first the psychical body of men and women, then the pneumatic body (against the Corinthian position that took the priority of the pneumatic body as axiomatic); so J. Jeremias—see note 9; (b) overlooks the flow of verse 44 to verse 46, with verse 45 as a scriptural proof brought in not to assert sequence but to state that new life comes only in Christ; (c) and fails to explain Paul's phrase "the second man [was] *from heaven.*" Only as Christ existed in heaven (his "preexistence") can he meaningfully be said to be "out of heaven" (*ex ouranou*: a parousia allusion? So Robertson-Plummer. He will come from heaven to bestow pneumatic bodies patterned on his "original" body as God's "image" or "form"—a prospect in view at verse 49, and developed in 15:50ff.). But the verbless phrase could just as well refer to Christ's original *Heimat* as a heavenly being; then it would stand in contrast to Adam's lowly origin "out of the earth" (Gen. 2:7). This

second interpretation is preferable if our subsequent discussion is on the right track. It argues that Paul is rebutting the false idea that Christ at his resurrection imparted new life to the Corinthian enthusiasts (v. 45), a conclusion Paul cites only to correct it by tracing back Christ's origin as *pneuma* to his life with God, to be shared with believers only after they have become "people-of-dust" as Adam was (v. 48). See earlier, p. 132.

It is strange that Dunn should conclude that "Paul explicitly *denies* that Christ precedes Adam" (p. 308 n. 41, his italics) when that point is exactly what Paul must make to establish that the resurrection bodies of Christians will resemble and share in Christ's "body of glory" (vv. 48, 49; Phil. 3:21) in the beginning. See further my critique in "Some Reflections on New Testament Hymns," in *Christ the Lord,* ed. H. H. Rowdon, 47f.

8. W. Eltester, *Eikon im Neuen Testament,* 23; see R. A. Horsley, "Pneumatikos vs. Psychikos," 269–88.

9. J. Jeremias, *"Adam,"* in *The Theological Dictionary of the New Testament,* 1:143.

10. There are several other places in 1 Corinthians where Paul's citation of his opponents' slogans has been suspected (e.g., 6:12=10:23; 6:13; 7:1; 8:1, 4, 5–6, 8; 11:2) as well as of the verses we have drawn attention to earlier (12:1, 31a; 14:1–5, 39). See J. C. Hurd, *The Origin of 1 Corinthians,* 67; and B. C. Johanson, "Tongues, A Sign for Unbelievers?" 180–203, especially 193f., who discusses 14:22 as representing—or at least reflecting—the Corinthian position on "tongues."

11. 1 Corinthians 15:51–52 is cast in oracular form (so identified by D. E. Aune, *Prophecy in Early Christianity and the Ancient Mediterranean World,* 250, 251), as is also 1 Thessalonians 4:15–17. If Paul is drawing upon a preformed writing, set in chiastic structure, it would be appropriate that he should use such a formula to combat the Corinthians' eschatological position by showing how death will result in the believers' new life, which must await the resurrection.

12. J. Jeremias, "'Flesh and Blood cannot Inherit the Kingdom of God,'" 151–59.

13. The positive side to this is the call to "excel in the work of the Lord" (v. 58). This verb (*perisseuein*) is a keyword in Paul's Corinthian correspondence (1 Cor. 8:8; 14:12; cf. 2 Cor. 3:9; 8:2, 7; 9:8, 12), and with its negative counterpart in 1:7 ("you *are lacking* no spiritual gift") it picks up the earlier debate over *charismata.* To the criteria of *agapē* and *oikodomē* as regulative of the spiritual gifts in Christ's body, Paul adds that Christian energies are deployed effectively only as they stand in the field of the risen power of Christ and point forward to the "not yet" of his future triumph.

BIBLIOGRAPHY

A. COMMENTARIES ON 1 CORINTHIANS

Allo, E. B. *(La) première épître aux Corinthiens*. Etudes bibliques. Paris: Gabalda, 1956.

Barrett, C. K. *The First Epistle to the Corinthians*. Harper-Black Commentaries. New York: Harper & Row, 1968.

Bruce, F. F. *1 and 2 Corinthians*. New Century Bible. London: Marshall, Morgan & Scott, 1971; Grand Rapids: Eerdmans, 1980.

Conzelmann, H. *1 Corinthians*. Hermeneia. Philadelphia: Fortress Press, 1975.

Godet, Frédéric. *Commentary on St. Paul's First Epistle to the Corinthians*. ET Edinburgh: T. & T. Clark, 1886–87.

Héring, J. *The First Epistle of Saint Paul to the Corinthians*. ET London: Epworth Press, 1962.

Lietzmann, H., and W. G. Kümmel. *An die Korinther I/II*. Handbuch z. NT. Tübingen: Mohr/Siebeck, 1949.

Moffatt, J. *The First Epistle of Paul to the Corinthians*. London: Hodder & Stoughton, 1938.

Morris, L. *1 Corinthians*. Tyndale New Testament Commentaries. London: Tyndale Press, 1963.

Robertson, A., and A. Plummer. *A Critical and Exegetical Commentary on the First Epistle of St. Paul to the Corinthians*. International Critical Commentary. Edinburgh: T. & T. Clark, 1914.

Senft, C. *La première épître de saint Paul aux Corinthiens*. Commentaire du Nouveau Testament. Neuchâtel: Delachaux et Niestlé, 1979.

Thrall, M. E. *1 and II Corinthians*. Cambridge Bible Commentary. Cambridge: Cambridge University Press, 1965.

Weiss, J. *Der erste Korintherbrief*. MeyerKommentar. Göttingen: Vandenhoeck & Ruprecht, 1910.

B. Other Works Cited*

[Arndt, W. F.], F. W. Gingrich, and F. W. Danker. *A Greek-English Lexicon of the New Testament and Other Early Christian Literature*. Chicago: University of Chicago Press, 1979 ed.

Aune, David E. *Prophecy in Early Christianity and the Ancient Mediterranean World*. Grand Rapids: Eerdmans, 1983.

Baillie, Donald M. *God was in Christ*. New York: C. Scribner's Sons, 1948.

*This list is restricted to titles referred to in the text, and does not include popular books and articles on both sides of the Pentecostal "divide."

Baird, William. *The Corinthian Church—A Biblical Approach to Urban Culture.* New York: Abingdon Press, 1964.

Baker, D. L. "The Interpretation of I Corinthians 12–14." *The Evangelical Quarterly* 46 (1974):224–34.

Banks, Robert. *Paul's Idea of Community.* Grand Rapids: Eerdmans, 1980.

Barclay, William. *New Testament Words.* London: SCM Press, 1974.

Barrett, C. K. *Essays on Paul.* Philadelphia: The Westminster Press, 1982.

Barth, Karl. *The Resurrection of the Dead.* ET New York: Fleming H. Revell, 1933.

_____. *Church Dogmatics* IV/2. ET Edinburgh: T. & T. Clark, 1958.

_____. *The Epistle to the Philippians.* ET London: SCM Press, 1962.

Bartling, W. J. "The Congregation of Christ: A Charismatic Body." *Concordia Theological Monthly* 40 (1969):67–80.

Bassler, J. M. "I Cor. 12:3—Curse and Confession in Context." *Journal of Biblical Literature* 101 (1982):415–21.

Beasley-Murray, George R. *Baptism in the New Testament.* New York: St. Martin's Press, 1962.

Best, Ernest. *One Body in Christ.* London: SPCK, 1955.

Beyschlag, K. "Clemens Romanus." *Beiträge zur historischen Theologie* 35 (1966).

Bittlinger, Arnold. *Gifts and Graces.* Grand Rapids: Eerdmans, 1968.

_____. *Gifts and Ministries.* Grand Rapids: Eerdmans, 1973.

Boman, T. "Paulus abortivus (1 Kor. 15,8)." *Studia Theologica* 18 (1964):46–50.

Bornkamm, Günther. *Early Christian Experience.* ET New York: Harper & Row, 1969.

Bradshaw, Paul F. *Daily Prayer in the Early Church.* London: Alcuin Club/SPCK, 1981.

Brandenburger, Egon. *Adam und Christus.* Neukirchen: Neukirchener Verlag, 1962.

Braun, H. "*perpereuomai.*" In *The Theological Dictionary of the New Testament.* Vol. 6. ET Grand Rapids: Eerdmans, 1968.

Brunner, Emil. *The Mediator.* ET Philadelphia: The Westminster Press, 1947.

Burkitt, Francis C. "On I Corinthians xv. 26." *Journal of Theological Studies* 17 (1916):384f.

Chadwick, H. "All Things to All Men." *New Testament Studies* 1 (1954–55):261–75.

Chevallier, Max-Alain. *Esprit de Dieu, Paroles d'Hommes.* Neuchâtel: Editions Delachaux et Niestlé, 1966.

Cranfield, C. E. B. "The Interpretation of I Peter iii. 19 and iv. 6." *The Expository Times* 69 (1958):365–72.

Cullmann, Oscar. *The Earliest Christian Confessions.* ET London: Lutter-worth Press, 1949.

———. *Christ and Time².* ET Philadelphia: The Westminster Press, 1950.

———. *The Christology of the New Testament.* ET Philadelphia: The West-minster Press, 1959.

———. *Salvation in History.* ET London: SCM Press, 1967.

Cuming, G. J. "*Epotisthēmen*: 1 Corinthians 12:13." *New Testament Studies* 27 (1981): 283–85.

de Lacey, D. R. "'One Lord' in Pauline Christology." In *Christ the Lord: Studies in Christology presented to Donald Guthrie,* edited by H. H. Rowdon. Downers Grove, IL: Inter-Varsity Press, 1982.

Denney, James. *The Way Everlasting.* London: Hodder and Stoughton, 1911.

Duncan, George S. *St. Paul's Ephesian Ministry.* New York: C. Scribner's Sons, 1930.

Dunn, James D. G. *Jesus and the Spirit.* Philadelphia: The Westminster Press, 1975.

———. *Christology in the Making.* Philadelphia: The Westminster Press, 1980.

Dykstra, W. "I Cor. 15:20–28: An Essential Part of Paul's Argument against those who deny the Resurrection?" *Calvin Theological Journal* 4 (1969): 195–211.

Ellis, E. Earle. *Paul's Use of the Old Testament.* Edinburgh: Oliver & Boyd, 1957.

———. *Prophecy and Hermeneutic in Early Christianity.* Tübingen: Mohr; Grand Rapids: Eerdmans, 1978.

Eltester, W. *Eikon im Neuen Testament.* Berlin: Töpelmann, 1958.

Engelsen, Nils Ivar Johan. *Glossolalia and Other Forms of Inspired Speech According to I Corinthians 12–14.* Thesis, Yale University, 1970; printed 1971.

Epp, E. J., and G. D. Fee, ed. *New Testament Textual Criticism.* B. M. Metzger Festschrift. Oxford: Clarendon Press, 1980.

Fee, Gordon D. "Tongues—Least of the Gifts? Some Exegetical Observations on I Corinthians 12–14." *Pneuma* 2 (1980):3–14.

Fridrichsen, Anton. *The Apostle and His Message.* Uppsala: Lundequistaka bokhandeln, 1947.

———. *The Problem of Miracle in Primitive Christianity.* ET Minneapolis: Augsburg Publishing House, 1972.

Friedrich, Gerhard. "*prophētēs*." In *The Theological Dictionary of the New Testament.* Vol. 6. ET Grand Rapids: Eerdmans, 1968.

Goldingay, John. *The Church and the Gifts of the Spirit.* Bamcote, Notts.: Grove Books, 1972.

Goodman, Felicitas D. *Speaking in Tongues: A Cross-Cultural Study of Glossolalia.* Chicago: University of Chicago Press, 1972.

Grudem, W. A. "A Response to Gerhard Dautzenberg on 1 Cor. 12:10." *Biblische Zeitschrift* 22 (1978):253–70.

―――. *The Gift of Prophecy in I Corinthians.* Washington, D.C.: University Press of America, 1982.

Gundry, Robert H. *SŌMA in Biblical Theology: with Emphasis on Pauline Anthropology.* New York: Cambridge University Press, 1976.

Güttgemanns, Erhardt. *Der leidende Apostel und sein Herr.* Göttingen: Vandenhoeck & Ruprecht, 1966.

Hengel, Martin. *Acts and the History of Earliest Christianity.* ET Philadelphia: Fortress Press, 1979.

―――. *The Charismatic Leader and His Followers.* ET New York: Crossroad, 1981.

Hill, David. *New Testament Prophecy.* Atlanta: John Knox Press, 1979.

Hollenweger, Walter J. *The Pentecostals.* Minneapolis: Augsburg Publishing House, 1972.

Horsley, R. A. "Pneumatikos vs. Psychikos." *Harvard Theological Review* 69 (1976):269–88.

House, H. Wayne. "Tongues and the Mystery Religions of Corinth." *Bibliotheca Sacra* 140 (1963):135–50.

Hurd, J. C. *The Origin of I Corinthians.* Macon, GA: Mercer Press, 1983 ed.

Hurley, James B. *Man and Woman in Biblical Perspective.* Grand Rapids: Zondervan, 1981.

Iber, G. "Zum Verständnis von I Cor. 12:31." *Zeitschrift für die neutestamentliche Wissenschaft* 54 (1963):43–52.

Isabell, C. D. "Glossolalia and Propheteialalia: A Study of I Cor. 14." *Wesley Theological Journal* 10 (1975):15–22.

Jansen, J. F. "1 Cor. 15:24–28." In *Texts and Testaments,* edited by W. E. March. San Antonio: Trinity University Press, 1980.

Jeremias, J. " 'Flesh and Blood cannot Inherit the Kingdom of God' (1 Cor. xv. 50)." *New Testament Studies* 2 (1955–56):151–59.

―――. "Adam." In *The Theological Dictionary of the New Testament.* Vol. 1. ET Grand Rapids: Eerdmans, 1964.

Johanson, B. C. "Tongues, A Sign for Unbelievers?" *New Testament Studies* 25 (1978–79):180–203.

Johansson, N. "I Cor. xiii and I Cor. xiv." *New Testament Studies* 10 (1963–64):383–92.

Johnson, Sherman E. "Paul in the Wicked City of Corinth." *Lexington Theological Quarterly* 17 (1982):59–67.

Käsemann, Ernst. *Leib und Leib Christi.* Tübingen: Mohr, 1933.

―――. *Essays on New Testament Themes.* Naperville, IL: Allenson, 1964.

_____. "Sentences of Holy Law in the New Testament." In *New Testament Questions of Today*. ET Philadelphia: Fortress Press, 1969.

_____. *Commentary on Romans*. ET Grand Rapids: Eerdmans, 1980.

Kim, Seyoon. *The Origin of Paul's Gospel*. Grand Rapids: Eerdmans, 1982.

Kloppenborg, J. "An Analysis of the Pre-Pauline Formula I Cor. 15:3b–5 in the Light of Some Recent Literature." *Catholic Biblical Quarterly* 40 (1978):351–67.

Koenig, John. *Charismata: God's Gifts for God's People*. Philadelphia: The Westminster Press, 1978.

Kramer, Werner. *Christ, Lord, Son of God*. ET Naperville, IL: Allenson, 1966.

Kümmel, Werner Georg. *Theology of the New Testament*. ET Nashville: Abingdon Press, 1973.

Künneth, Walter. *The Theology of the Resurrection*. ET St. Louis: Concordia Publishing House, 1965.

Ladd, George Eldon. *A Theology of the New Testament*. Grand Rapids: Eerdmans, 1974.

Lane, William L. "I Timothy iv. 1–3. An Early Instance of Over-Realized Eschatology?" *New Testament Studies* 11 (1964–65):164–67.

Layton, B., ed. *The Gnostic Treatise on Resurrection from Nag Hammadi*. Missoula, MT: Scholars Press, 1979.

Lincoln, A. T. *Paradise Now and Not Yet*. New York: Cambridge University Press, 1981.

Lindars, Barnabas. *New Testament Apologetic*. Philadelphia: The Westminster Press, 1961.

Lohmeyer, Ernst. *Der Brief an die Philipper*. 9th ed. Göttingen: Vandenhoeck & Ruprecht, 1953.

_____. *Kyrios Jesus: Eine Untersuchung zu Phil 2,5–11*. 2nd ed. Heidelberg: Carl Winter, 1961.

Lohse, Eduard. *Colossians and Philemon*. ET Hermeneia. Philadelphia: Fortress Press, 1971.

MacDonald, Dennis R. *The Legend and the Apostle*. Philadelphia: The Westminster Press, 1983.

MacGorman, Jack W. *The Gifts of the Spirit: An Exposition of I Corinthians 12–14*. Nashville: Broadman, 1974.

Malherbe, Abraham J. "The Beasts at Ephesus." *Journal of Biblical Literature* 87 (1968):71–80.

Martin, Ralph P. "A Suggested Exegesis of I Corinthians 13:13." *The Expository Times* 82 (1970–71):119–20.

_____. *New Testament Foundations*. Vols. 1 and 2. Grand Rapids: Eerdmans, 1975, 1978.

_____. *The Family and the Fellowship*. Grand Rapids: Eerdmans, 1980.

_____. *Colossians and Philemon*. New Century Bible. London: Marshall, Morgan & Scott, 1973; Grand Rapids: Eerdmans, 1981.

_____. *Reconciliation: A Study of Paul's Theology*. Atlanta: John Knox Press, 1981.

_____. *The Worship of God: Some Theological, Pastoral, and Practical Reflections*. Grand Rapids: Eerdmans, 1982.

_____. "Some Reflections on New Testament Hymns." In *Christ the Lord. Essays on Christology Presented to Donald Guthrie*, edited by H. H. Rowdon. Downers Grove, IL: Inter-Varsity, 1982.

_____. "New Testament Hymns: Background and Development." *The Expository Times* 94 (1983):132–36.

Marxsen, Willi. *The Resurrection of Jesus of Nazareth*. ET Philadelphia: Fortress Press, 1970.

Meeks, Wayne A. *The First Urban Christians. The Social World of the Apostle Paul*. New Haven: Yale University Press, 1983.

Metzger, B. M. "A Suggestion Concerning the Meaning of I Cor. xv. 4b." *Journal of Theological Studies* 8 (1957):118–23.

Moule, H. C. G. *The Cross and the Spirit*. London: Pickering & Inglis, n.d.

Moulton, James H., and Nigel Turner. *A Grammar of the New Testament Greek*. Vol. 3. Edinburgh: T. & T. Clark, 1963.

Müller, Ulrich B. *Prophetie und Predigt im Neuen Testament*. Gütersloh: Gütersloher Verlagshaus Mohn, 1975.

Munck, J. "Paulus tanquam abortivus." In *New Testament Essays in Memory of T. W. Manson*, edited by A. J. B. Higgins, 180–93. Manchester: Manchester University Press, 1959.

Murphy-O'Connor, J. "Tradition and Redaction in I Cor. 15:3–7." *Catholic Biblical Quarterly* 43 (1981):583–89.

_____. *St. Paul's Corinth. Texts and Archaeology*. Wilmington, Delaware: M. Glazier, Inc., 1983.

Neill, Stephen. *The Christian Faith Today*. Harmondsworth, Middlesex: Penguin Books, 1955.

Neuhaus, Richard J. *Freedom for Ministry*. San Francisco: Harper & Row, 1979.

O'Neill, J. C. "I Corinthians 15:29." *The Expository Times* 91 (1980): 310–11.

Painter, John. "Paul and the *Pneumatikoi* at Corinth." In *Paul and Paulinism: Essays in Honour of C. K. Barrett*, edited by M. D. Hooker and S. G. Wilson. London: SPCK, 1982.

Pearson, B. A. *The Pneumatikos—Psychikos Terminology in I Corinthians*. Missoula, MT: SBL Monograph series, 1973.

Pederson, Sigfred. "Agape—der eschatologische Hauptbegriff bei Paulus." In *Die paulinische Literatur und Theologie*, edited by S. Pederson. Arhus: Forlaget Aros, 1980.

Plank, K. A. "Resurrection Theology: The Corinthian Controversy Re-examined." *Perspectives in Religious Studies* 8 (1981):41–54.

Raeder, Marie. "Vikariastaufe in I Cor. 15,29?" *Zeitschrift für die neutesta-mentliche Wissenschaft* 46 (1955):258–60.

Riesenfeld, Harald. "Note sur I Cor. 13." *Coniectanea Neotestamentica* 10 (1946):2f.

―――. "Vorbildliches Martyrium." *Donum Gentilicum. New Testament Studies in Honour of David Daube,* edited by E. Bammel, C. K. Barrett, and W. D. Davies. Oxford: Clarendon, 1978.

Rissi, Matthias. *Die Taufe für die Toten.* Zürich: Zwingli Verlag, 1962.

Robinson, D. W. B. "*Charismata* versus *Pneumatika.* Paul's Method of Discussion." *Reformed Theological Review* 31 (1972):49–55.

Robinson, John A. T. *The Body. A Study in Pauline Theology.* London: SCM Press, 1952.

Schlatter, Adolf. *Paulus, der Bote Jesu.* Stuttgart: Calwer, 1934.

Schmithals, W. *Gnosticism in Corinth.* ET Nashville: Abingdon, 1971.

Schniewind, J. "Die Leugnung der Auferstehung in Korinth." In *Nachgelassene Reden und Aufsätze,* edited by Erich Kahler. Berlin: Töpelmann, 1952.

Schrage, W. "Leid, Kreuz und Eschaton." *Evangelische Theologie* 34 (1974):141–75.

Schütz, J. H. *Paul and the Anatomy of Apostolic Authority.* Cambridge: Cambridge University Press, 1975.

Schweitzer, Albert. *The Mysticism of the Apostle Paul.* ET London: A. & C. Black, 1931.

Schweizer, Eduard. "Worship in the New Testament." *The Reformed and Presbyterian World* 24 (1957). Reprinted in *Neotestamentica, German and English Essays 1951–63.* Zurich: Zwingli Verlag, 1963.

―――. "Der Glaube an Jesus den 'Herrn' in seiner Entwicklung von den ersten Nachfolgern bis zur hellenistischen Gemeinde." *Evangelische Theologie* 17 (1957):7–21.

―――. "The Church as the Missionary Body of Christ." *New Testament Studies* 8 (1961–62):1–11.

―――. *Church Order in the New Testament.* ET London: SCM Press, 1961.

―――. "*pneuma.*" In *The Theological Dictionary of the New Testament.* Vol. 6. ET Grand Rapids: Eerdmans, 1968.

―――. "*sarx.*" In *The Theological Dictionary of the New Testament.* Vol. 7. ET Grand Rapids: Eerdmans, 1971.

―――. *The Holy Spirit.* ET Philadelphia: Fortress Press, 1980.

Scroggs, R. "Paul and the Eschatological Woman." *Journal of the American Academy of Religion* 40.3 (1972):283–303.

Sevenster, Jan Nicholaas. *Paul and Seneca.* Leiden: E. J. Brill, 1961.

Smedes, Lewis B. *Love Within Limits.* Grand Rapids: Eerdmans, 1978.

Smith, D. Moody. "Glossolalia and Other Spiritual Gifts in a NT Perspective." *Interpretation* 28 (1974):307–20.

Stendahl, Krister. *The Bible and the Role of Women.* Philadelphia: Fortress Press, 1966.

———. *Paul Among Jews and Gentiles.* Philadelphia: Fortress Press, 1977.

Sweet, J. M. "A Sign for Unbelievers." *New Testament Studies* 13 (1966–67):240–57.

Theissen, Gerd. *The Social Setting of Pauline Christianity: Essays on Corinth.* ET Philadelphia: Fortress Press, 1982.

Thiselton, A. C. "The 'Interpretation' of Tongues." *Journal of Theological Studies* 30 (1979): 15–36.

Thompson, K. C. "I Corinthians 15,29 and Baptism for the Dead." *Studia Evangelica* 2.1 (1964):647–59.

Toews, J. E. "The Role of Women in the Church: A Pauline Perspective." *Direction* 9.1 (1980):25–35.

Usami, K. "How are the Dead Raised?" *Biblica* 51 (1976):468–93.

von Allmen, J. J. *Worship: Its Theology and Practice.* New York: Oxford University Press, 1965.

von Harnack, A. *The Mission and Expansion of Christianity in the First Three Centuries.* Vol. 1. ET New York: G. P. Putnam's Sons, 1908.

von Rad, Gerhard. "Die Vorgeschichte der Gattung von 1 Cor. 13,4–7." In *Geschichte und Altes Testament Festschrift für A. Alt.* Tübingen: Mohr, 1953, 153–68. ET: "The Early History of the Form-Category of I Corinthians xiii. 4–7." In *The Problem of the Hexateuch.* Edinburgh and London: Oliver & Boyd, 1965, 301–17.

Watson, David C. *I Believe in the Church.* Grand Rapids: Eerdmans, 1978.

Wedderburn, A. J. M. "The Problem of the Denial of the Resurrection in I Cor. xv." *Novum Testamentum* 23 (1981):229–41.

Wegenast, Klaus. *Das Verständnis der Tradition bei Paulus und in den Deuteropaulinen.* Neukirchen: Neukirchener, 1962.

Williams, Cyril G. *Tongues of the Spirit: A Study of Pentecostal Glossolalia and Related Phenomena.* Cardiff: Cardiff University Press, 1981.

Wilson, R. McL. "Gnosis at Corinth." In *Paul and Paulinism: Essays in Honour of C. K. Barrett,* edited by M. D. Hooker and S. G. Wilson. London: SPCK, 1982.

Wischmeyer, Oda. *Der höchste Weg. Das 13. Kapitel des 1. Korintherbriefes.* Gütersloh: Gütersloher Verlagshaus, 1981.

Zuntz, Günther. *The Text of the Epistles.* London: Published for the British Academy by Oxford University Press, 1953.

INDEXES

I. Principal Subjects

Paul: as authority, 4; conversion of, 23, 25, 92, 93, 99–101; as pastor, 3, 4, 30, 121, 122, 142, 143; preaching of, 93, 101, 102, 109
Philanthropy, 44
Plato, 22, 26
Praise, 60, 61, 70–74
Prophets, prophecy, 9, 14, 32, 33, 53, 56, 62, 65–68, 73, 79, 80
Praying, 69–70

Resurrection, viii, 88, 91–94, 109, 118–25; newness of, 138–42; priority of, 134–38; rationale of, 131–34

Salvation-History, 110–18
Sacrifice, 45
Seneca, 22
Spiritual gifts, 7, 8, 34. *See also* Charismatic gifts
Stoics, 22, 23, 28, 29

Teacher, teaching, 32, 33, 87, 88, 138
Tongues, 33, 43, 69, 71, 72, 77, 78, 83, 85, 88, 130, 148, 154. *See also* Glossolalia

Upbuilding, 3, 19, 44, 46, 61, 62, 66, 78, 154

Wisdom, 13, 36, 41

II. Modern Authors

Allo, E. B., 81
Aune, D. E., 81, 146, 150, 154

Baillie, D. M., 100, 152
Baird, W., 12, 94, 146, 147, 151
Baker, D. L., 34, 147
Banks, R., 30, 147
Barclay, W., 48, 148
Barrett, C. K., 10, 23, 28, 29, 30, 32, 42, 51, 62, 69, 79, 81, 85, 91, 92, 104, 109, 115, 116, 117, 145, 146, 147, 152
Barth, K., 3, 43, 46, 116, 123, 145, 147, 148, 153
Bartling, W. J., 147
Bassler, J. M., 145
Beasley-Murray, G. R., 153
Best, E., 18, 28, 29, 147
Beyschlag, K., 45, 147
Bittlinger, A., 11, 14, 18, 34, 84, 146, 147, 150
Boman, T., 92, 151
Bornkamm, G., 46, 147
Bradshaw, P. F., 60, 61, 148
Brandenburger, E., 131, 153
Braun, H., 48, 148

Bruce, F. F., 11, 13, 14, 42, 51, 53, 73, 81, 85, 91, 104, 123, 146, 151
Brunner, E., 102, 152
Burkitt, F. C., 116, 152

Chadwick, H., 149
Chevallier, M.-A., 34, 36, 65, 66, 71, 147, 148, 149
Conzelmann, H., 19, 20, 21, 28, 42, 43, 51, 58, 75, 81, 84, 91, 93, 95, 97, 101, 104, 111, 132, 135, 137, 153
Cranfield, C. E. B., 152
Cullmann, O., 110, 117, 152
Cuming, G. J., 147

Danker, F. W., 39, 150
de Lacey, D. R., 149
Denney, J., 19, 55, 146, 148
Duncan, G. S., 122, 153
Dunn, J. D. G., 66, 67, 68, 70, 81, 86, 128, 134, 148, 149, 150, 153, 154
Dykstra, W., 152

III. *Scriptural References*